the company culture cookbook

the company culture cookbook

how to change the way we do things around here

kevin m. thomson

FINANCIAL TIMES
Prentice Hall

an imprint of Pearson Education

London • New York • Toronto • Sydney • Tokyo • Singapore • Hong Kong • Cape Town
New Delhi • Madrid • Paris • Amsterdam • Munich • Milan • Stockholm

PEARSON EDUCATION LIMITED

Head Office:
Edinburgh Gate
Harlow CM20 2JE
Tel: +44 (0)1279 623623
Fax: +44 (0)1279 431059

London Office:
128 Long Acre
London WC2E 9AN
Tel: +44 (0)20 7447 2000
Fax: +44 (0)20 7240 5771
Websites: www.business-minds.com
　　　　　www.thecompanyculturecookbook.com

_____

First published in Great Britain in 2002

© Kevin Thomson 2002

The right of Kevin Thomson to be identified as Author
of this Work has been asserted by him in accordance
with the Copyright, Designs and Patents Act 1988.

Photographs courtesy of GettyImages Creative and Corbis UK

ISBN 0 273 65661 9

British Library Cataloguing in Publication Data
A CIP catalogue record for this book can be obtained from the British Library

10 9 8 7 6 5 4 3 2 1

Typeset by Pantek Arts Ltd, Maidstone, Kent
Printed and bound by Rotolito Lombardo, Italy

The Publishers' policy is to use paper manufactured from sustainable forests.

dedicated to a great guy who knew how to get an organization cooking

This book is dedicated to someone who I only knew for a few short months before he tragically died. In that brief time he became someone who stays in my heart as the epitome of a leader, boss, customer and friend to many. A man who knew how to change cultures by leading by example of what he did, what he said and how he looked when he was doing it. I hope he is still holding those wow! meetings making those around him stand on the board room table in heaven.

to Greg Fallon (formerly President, Novell EMEA)

contents

*indicates exercises

contents

part 2: the sixteen personalities around the table 152

part 3: the six critical success factors 204

addendum: everything has changed 216

all the guests are going home ... 241

prologue

This book was written, as a labor of love, during the year before September 11 2001. Yet even after the massive changes this day and its aftermath has meant for many organizations, from changes in security to large-scale redundancy and re-structuring, I have decided not to change any of the recipes, nor indeed the "fun" nature of the book. I have decided only to add an addendum "food to feed the spirit." This addendum was written first, to help people deal with specific issues around crisis communication and second, to give ideas and examples for handling some of the difficult issues concerning the personal, economic, political, and social fallout we have all seen since then, and may continue to see for many years to come.

But surely "everything has changed" – so is an addendum on crisis or conflict enough? Should not the whole book have changed with its fun approach, its "tongue in cheek" style, and bold outlook? Yes, I believe everything has changed for businesses, brands, employees, customers, and consumers, not least of which is our personal and financial security, and the now accelerated trend of how we view our lives both inside and outside work. And yet I believe that what you will be reading, about the changing of culture inside companies, is not just as important for today, for tomorrow, or the day after, I believe that the changes I have written about will become infinitely more important from now on.

The "recipes" in *the company culture cookbook* have been created, tried, and tested over the 20 years I have focussed on internal marketing, branding, and communication, working with many of the world's most exciting and successful organizations, both large and small, long established and new. The book however was written at a time when "change" was a goal in itself for most organizations and the recipes became an analogy to help people change. The recipes became an analogy to help people change not what they think, feel, and believe, for that had been tried and too often failed (with us all going through years and years of "visions, missions, and values") but to change behaviors, words and deeds. In short, a recipe to change the way we change.

Why do we need to change the way we change? Because organizational change, of itself, and as a goal of business, is no longer enough to excite people in the work place, to motivate them to want to succeed or even deliver. Now we live in a time when everyone at work recognizes that crisis, conflict, and global consciousness of the world we live in, as well as our own personal way we create our life/work balance, must be as much a part of the way we do things, as the day-to-day running and "changing" of the business. The way we deal with our life in work must now reflect this exciting and challenging world we live in.

So now, as you read each recipe, please reflect on the desire that everyone has to live, breathe, and work in an environment that gladdens the heart, helps the mind to soar, feeds the spirit, and enriches the soul. And all this in an atmosphere that inspires us to laugh, to smile, to giggle, to invent, to lead, to manage, to improve, to change, to grow, and to care that everything we do has an impact on all those around us – at work, at home, and abroad, in this increasingly small world of ours.

kevin m. thomson
the executive chef

small

world

faith

passion

pride

a change for the better

by Lord Marshall, Chairman, British Airways

With a century of rulebook management behind us, the time must be right for the blandness of traditional administration to be spiced with more creative and more exciting ingredients. If we accept that continuous business change is inevitable in a global economy, then the first important step of management is removal of the fear of change. The really successful companies of the 21st century will be those where change is not imposed from the top down, but created from the bottom up.

To build a creative, enterprising workforce, business environments need to reflect the way people live their lives in this day and age; and if I was asked to describe in one word the factor which distinguishes our top companies and top managers from the rest, I would offer "excitement."

When you think about it, that is the job of management – to excite markets, to excite shareholders and – crucially – to excite employees. This is why British Airways has worked with Kevin Thomson and his team over the last three years on the "Putting People First Again" program. More than 50,000 of our people attended the series of one-day courses which featured team working; brand awareness break out sessions; and customer-driven "brand ambassador" discussions. The program, coupled with its award-winning video productions, did help to re-invigorate British Airways with a sense of excitement.

Research shows that implementation of "PPFA" raised the "emotional capital" of our people across the world. It built greater customer awareness, deepened company loyalty, and improved morale – with a tangible effect on the bottom line.

Pride, passion, and faith among employees are some of the secret ingredients Kevin discusses in this book. We re-kindled these emotions in our business and they made a difference as we faced tough times. I believe they are core elements to any successful business strategy, but they are very easy to lose and hard to regenerate.

Why does business need to change through people, rather than in spite of them? We are moving from a century of control management to a new era of creativity, ideas, delivery, and excitement owned and shared by all. The line between what happens outside work and what occurs within the company is becoming blurred. We have to build and sustain great brands for our external customers; and must do the same for the internal market, our people.

Nowadays, if we want effective change we should not simply serve it up on a plate, but give people the ingredients to complete the dish themselves. To create is to own – and ownership produces pride, commitment, and excitement.

Here, then, is a recipe to new ways of creating the menu of excitement your business should be presenting to its customers.

enjoy *the company culture cookbook*

Lord Marshall of Knightsbridge
Chairman, British Airways

a message from the executive chef

Not once, not twice, not just some of the time, but over and over and over, at conferences, with clients and when conducting research with people in organizations from all over the world I am asked: "Yes, we know we have to change our culture, but how?"

This is the question that this book sets out to answer "How do we change culture?" But not in the way you might think. For I believe that an organization's culture, or what people THINK, FEEL, and BELIEVE is the *output* of any change process, not the input. This gives us our first problem, that you can't change culture – not directly. Culture I define as the *result* of everything that happens when you get together with others and interact with them. You end up thinking, feeling, and believing whatever you do only when you have seen, heard, or touched whatever you did.

So instead of focussing on the output of change, *the company culture cookbook* focusses on what I believe are the *inputs* of change.The good thing for you is that the inputs that will help you change your culture are really simple to understand and simple to do (maybe hard work, but simple) – and herein lies the strength and beauty of tackling culture change like this. For the way to ultimately change culture is to change what you SAY, what you DO, and how you LOOK. Call them "behaviors," call the process "behavioral change" if it helps you to highlight the difference with for example "attitudinal change." These behaviors and the visual and verbal inputs, or more simply the things that can be observed and heard, are what I define as the climate. The climate of any organization is best summed up in that wonderful phrase "the way we do things around here." And it is *only* when the climate changes, for the better (or worse), will culture be affected.

The second problem with culture change is the way we go about it; we try and change culture corporately (another strategic imperative coming up), in a way that is often complex (change "initiatives" coming out of our ears), mostly "top down" (here are our vision, missions, and values – now get on with it) sometimes dull (not another slide presentation), usually never ending (this is our 14th change program – in 14 months) and another change with yet another change of leadership (with the average length of CEO measured in days/months not years). Is there a better way?

What about giving every individual, *starting with you*, a way of changing which is fun, exciting, different, challenging, yet is simple to understand, requires only a little more time, needs just a bit more hard work, maybe lots of repetition to make it stick, yet above all is practical and pragmatic?

When I thought of writing a book on the subject – the "how to..." everyone had asked for – I wanted to create a new way of looking at how we "walk the talk"; a new way of doing things differently; a new way to change the way we do things around here. I browsed through a raft of management books, each of varying length from 50,000 to 150,000 words. I felt bombarded by words, words, words, words interspersed with models, graphs, charts and more words of explanation. "There has to be a better way," I said to myself. It didn't take long to find it. Eureka! A full display of the top selling book of the moment, *The River Café Cook Book*. My favorite lunchtime restaurant. Here in a beautifully presented, glossy, tantalizing, visually exciting book, wrapped in a terrific bold, bright green cover was a veritable feast of photography and quick, easy to follow recipes. The world over, individuals buy recipe books with pictures. Why? Because recipes are the quintessential "how to's" and the photographs entice people to try them.

My thanks to the authors of *The River Café Cook Book*. They have given me the most priceless ingredient of all – inspiration. Like its culinary counterpart, *the company culture cookbook* aims to be practical and simple; it gives you recipes to help you DO things differently, SAY things differently, and a way to LOOK different to affect your climate. In turn you will see, hear, and feel the difference in your culture as people start to THINK, FEEL, and BELIEVE in a way that is unique to your company or organization!

food

for thought

a feast of how to's

here are just some of the ways *the company culture cookbook* can help you develop your business, your performance, and your people, worldwide

- **from climate to culture**
  How to move from the old focus of changing culture to creating an exciting new climate.

- **from beliefs to behaviors**
  How to change beliefs by changing behaviors. To change what people THINK and FEEL and BELIEVE, you have to change your behaviors, what you SAY, what you DO, and how you LOOK.

- **from emotional valueS to economic valuE**
  How to capture hearts and minds to deliver on the bottom line. By creating emotional valueS in your business and your brand, you add economic valuE to your balance sheet and share price.

- **from visions that no-one sees to "I see...." says the leader
  – and everyone else sees too**
  How to get your vision for your organization across to those who so far may not be listening so that "I see…" becomes "We see it too!" Research and experience shows that staff in organizations rarely understand let alone believe in the "big picture" and do not trust the leaders. If this vision stuff isn't working now… DO something different!

- **from ideas to innovation**
  How to turn creativity into revenue. In today's ever changing market, new, new, new means new, new, new ways of doing it. Here's a new menu for innovation that works.

- **from corporate megaphone to dynamic dialogue**
  How to stop "talking at" and go about "listening to" by questioning and gaining understanding in a way that generates relationships and adds value to businesses and the people in them.

- **from employees to internal customers**
  From looking at your employees as one mass market to looking at everyone as an individual, just like internal customers, each with their own personality profile.

- **from one recipe to a book full of them**
  From one recipe that says "Do it like this (or else)" to a cook book that lets everyone create the kind of organization you want.

- **the bottom line**
  the company culture cookbook is a new way of approaching business that lets you DO it differently, SAY it differently, LOOK different when you do it. That's when you will see, hear, and feel the difference you can make.

an overview of the three parts

part 1 the six menus for a change

plus **the secret ingredients** ● **the red hot peppers**
the poison mushrooms ● **chef's notes**

the six menus for a change

The company culture cookbook is one big "how to"; how to change the SAY, DO, LOOK of your business. By changing these behaviors, I believe you gradually change what people THINK, FEEL, and BELIEVE to ensure your business stays ahead. The six menus for a change each contain various courses, with a total of over 40 recipes and special side dishes.

Using our culinary analogy, each of our six menus parallels the main components of business change that ultimately affect culture. These are the critical issues of leadership ("Great bosses!"), innovation ("Our customers love our new stuff!"), managing (getting high performance), communicating (getting buy-in), questioning (what questions do you ask?) and saying thank you (whilst saving money at the same time). The menus will help you create the right environment in which you and those around you work. This is what I call the climate. In real life, it is the climate, from arctic conditions to tropical rain forests, which creates the conditions in which people have adapted and built their cultures.

In organizational life the climate, coming from our words, the SAY, our deeds, the DO, and our manners and appearance, the LOOK, produces the feelings and beliefs within the individual, and in turn collectively within the company. It is how we walk the talk that produces the many and varied cultures in organizations. It is these differing climates that create differing cultures and this in turn has a profound impact on the success of an organization.

the secret ingredients

As a bonus there are also some secret ingredients that are worth a fortune if you use them correctly: these secret ingredients are called emotions. They are secret because they are hidden in your people's hearts and are ingredients because they create the environment you have now, and without some of them you won't be able to create the culture you really want.

the red hot peppers

The red hot peppers are the negative counterpart to positive emotions. Be very, very careful with these for they will kill the taste of anything – even if slightly over used.

the poison mushrooms

Watch out they are everywhere. Some of them look innocuous but they are deadly.

chef's notes
I have added the chef's notes to help you through the book and to give you guidelines to help you create positive changes in your organization.

time for something different

part 2 the sixteen personalities around the table

A good meal needs something more than a venue and food; it needs the people around the table to start doing and saying things that make the meal memorable. So, what is it about the people that make some meals work well, where the mix is perfect, the conversation delightful, the company wonderful, and others such a disaster?

what makes people tick?

the personality traits, their "shapes and shades"

This section gives you the ultimate personality "how to," to work out who is like what and why. "Shapes and shades" is the fastest and most fun psychometric test in the world; it's simple, easy, and user-friendly. It explains how the colors and designs people choose can help you understand them and communicate more effectively with them using *their* preferred style – not yours!

who works best with whom?

the "personality planner"

The "personality planner" is a quick reference grid for working out who has what personality type. You will find out how many of the eight personality traits you have in total in the team. From there you will have the questions to ask about how to maximize the strengths of the individuals and the team.

how do you find the right mix of personalities?

the types – a character complementer

The character complementer comes from using the eight personality traits to create for you the descriptions of the 16 types of people you will find in every walk of life. By understanding who is what type, you will be able to maximize their potential and also create the right mix with others. (Oh, and one unknown personality. There's always one.)

part 3 the six critical success factors

three checks on climate and culture and one yes! factor

You need to know if the recipes and your table planning have created the right results. How will you find out? By asking the right questions. Six questions are posed, three for checking your climate in terms of what your people say, do, and how they look when they are interacting day in, day out, and three for checking the impact of the climate on your culture in terms of what people think, feel, and believe.

As a final feel good check, this is the ultimate test – the yes! factor. It's instant, visual, verbal, visceral, and palpable.

addendum: everthing has changed

food to feed the spirit

I have added this chapter as a result of the events on September 11 2001.

visit www.thecompanyculturecookbook.com

You've got the book, now do the "personality pairs" online, for you and your friends/team/colleagues – and a whole lot more to SAY/DO/LOOK AT besides.

---

chef's notes
The recipes "at a glance" are displayed on the next pages.

who's coming to dinner?

10	13	15	17	19
he secret ingredients	think feel believe	obsession	challenge	passion

31	33	34	37	39
desire	trust	the red hot peppers	fear	anger

53	55	57	59	61
body language	eye ... contact	knock-out looks	hand signals	it's the way we do things around here

75	77	79	81	83
yes... and...	imagine if...	thinking out of the box	no, no's	no... but...

95	97	99	101	103
his is going to make me famous	all it takes	never again	innovating inside the box	the four f's

104
ready, steady, go!

108
managing in fast companies

111
all go!

113
fast...forward

115
no pain?
no gain!

129
what! questions?

131
so, what

133
moving up

136
communicating

139
why talk?

155
me... creative?

157
fill me in

164
the character complementer

167
the boss

169
the loose cannon!

181
guardian angel

183
the friend in need

185
the coach

187
the supporter

189
the rock

204
part 3: the six critical
success factors

207
what's up?

209
are you boiling over?

211
too hot to handle

213
yes!

117
didits and goforits

119
bless you

121
what's good
what could be better

123
don't say I can't

126
questioning

142
saying thank you

145
thanks Chip!

147
it's my pleasure

149
more smiles

152
part 2: the sixteen
personalities around the table

171
the thinker

173
the investigator

175
the helper

177
the butterfly

179
the watcher

191
the sorter

193
the fixer

195
the bystander

197
the pragmatist

199
the unknown

215
future... over to you

all the guests are
going home

216
addendum:
everything has changed

240
the next generation

Kevin Thomson
author

enjoy your meal!

mwaahh!

the first menu –
leading into the future
when you need to deliver the vision thing

menu

talk the talk –
the verbal language of leadership

As a leader, what you say matters. It's one of the key contributors to a positive or negative climate and culture. So it pays to watch what you say, and think hard about its impact on your organization...

- "KILL the competition."
- "We'd better grab more market share, NOW! (or else)."
- "This quarter revenue/profit/share price/motivation is down, what are YOU going to do about it?"

Is this the language of leadership in your organization? Is it masculine, militaristic, tough, top-down, profit-driven, figures-orientated, hard-hitting, accusatory, angry, LOUD?

What's wrong with that, or even some of that? Maybe nothing if the majority in your organization is motivated by masculine, militaristic, hard-hitting language – often articulated in instructions sent down from "on high." If you talk, walk, look like a military leader then guess what climate you'll create and guess what culture will result?

Is this the language of leadership in the 21st century? No. Sometimes hard-hitting language can be a strength: however, too much of a strength will become a weakness.

So what is the language of leadership? It comes in three parts: what you SAY, what you DO, and how you LOOK. What follows are the words, deeds, and actions you can take to lead the change in your climate.

chef's notes

Let's start with the "big picture"...the vision, mission, and values.

How do we turn often lifeless corporate jargon and meaningless rhetoric into powerful motivating words?

By changing the *language* of your vision, mission, and values, and mixing it together with the secret ingredients – our emotions.

Once we have clarified and distilled the "talk the talk" you can move into what you DO to "walk the walk"; then you can ensure the way you LOOK fixes the story you are saying into the fabric of your organization – the "look the look" as I call it. For surely leadership is about leading – by words and deeds and actions.

say do look

I see –
vision, a really personal thing

ingredients

A vision comes from somebody, a person with foresight, a leader who "sees" into the future. When it comes to visions I believe that the two words "I see…" are the ingredients that produce the most important words of all for a leader. Sounds too simple? How many visions do staff, customers, investors, the community "see" that are linked to a living, breathing, feeling leader and how many visions sit in dull documents, on posters, or on give-away gadgets?

The more personal a leader is when it comes to what they THINK, FEEL, and BELIEVE, the more likely people are to follow them. It is when they "buy" you the person, that they will follow the vision itself. I believe that both the leader and their vision need marketing – both to internal and external customers. What do you have to SAY, DO, and how do you have to LOOK to get across your hidden desire? You say "I see…"

It's obviously not OK to say the "I" word as a boast: "I did this." "I said that." "I got them to do the other." However, when it comes to visions, I believe that it's not just OK to use the "I" word, it's what people want. People want to see what *you* see.

Great leaders take responsibility for their vision; for their decisions; for their people. If, as the leader, you only get across "I see…" that's almost your leadership role accomplished! Then of course you need to support everyone else to do what needs to be done, starting with the board, your team, your colleagues, and whoever else you have in and around your organization (see *missions*, the next recipe). By taking this responsibility then I believe you will be seen as a leader, not a manager.

method

What will you SAY to inspire people?

- "I see…"
- "I'm looking forward to the time when our business and brand are recognized as…"
- "I believe that our organization is heading for exciting and profitable times where the goods and services we provide will…"
- "I see the future where…"
- "I am proud to lead an organization where I believe we will…"
- "I know that we face tough times ahead, I know the markets are changing, I know technology is forcing us to alter everything we do. I also know that we will succeed in achieving our goals of…"

chef's notes

The "talk the talk" by any leader can be strong, can be powerful, and *must* be very personal. Think of all the great leaders in the past. It was the individuals first and their words second, that caused people to follow them. I believe this with all my heart. I see a time when many more people will believe it too.

my vision

we are/we do –
a mission is a very public thing

A mission is a cause which unites and inspires a group of people to action. Think of the original missionaries. Think of the disciples; to start with, there were just 12 of them. They went out and soon there were MILLIONS. A mission requires ownership, commitment, passion, and trust.

ingredients

Whilst the language of a vision is a very personal thing, the language of a mission is a very public thing. Whilst the language of visions needs to be the language of "I see..." the language of missions needs to be the language of "We are/We do..."

method

Take your current mission statement and try using this language, SAY any combination of:

- "We are/we do..."
- "We are an organization dedicated to..."
- "We fundamentally believe that the future of XYZ lies with..."
- "We are constantly striving to ensure..."
- "We have worked for over 100 years for the good of our community and our goal is to work for the next 100 years to..."
- "We have established our reputation as the number one in ABC. Our mission is to stay that way for the next..."
- "We may be small, but we..."

"We try harder!" A great (only) three words mission statement from Avis recognized the world over. The word "we" is first and takes up one third of the whole statement. The rest sums up what they are – an organization that tries harder. Enough said – in three words.

chef's notes

"*We* are..." Why is the word "we" important? For that we have to go back in time to something "we" have forgotten. The basis of the word company is that of a company of *people*. In other words, people coming together for a common purpose – to make, build, do something, and/or go somewhere. Why? Because they *want* to. A company is the point at which "I" turns into "we." Sadly the concept of a "company" (often linked to "limited" or "public") has been reduced to one of a financial entity measured in profit and loss, assets and liabilities, not an emotional entity.

A "company" is so much more than a financial entity; it is a group of people coming together to share their hopes, their dreams, their fundamental need for human contact. All this can be expressed in the word "we." Yet how often have senior management teams struggled with the words of what they do and missed a simple word "we" to demonstrate who will do it?

When you do communicate a vision people can "see" and a mission they want to follow you have a recipe for success. One to inspire and enable 12, 120, 1,200, 12,000, or 120,000 people – or whatever the size of your organization – to do or be whatever you and they want to do or be.

our mission

what's important –
creating valuE from valueS

ingredients

Have you ever stopped to consider that the word values contains the word value? We talk about them as two separate and often very different words. Often strategy, finance, operations, people talk about valuE (as in economic value or added value) and human resources, communication, and marketing people talk about valueS (like business values and brand values). And yet value sits inside values; a powerful combination of human and financial factors. But what do we DO? We treat them separately, discuss them separately, and give them to different departments to deal with – separately.

Surely any recipe helping deliver values needs to be adding wealth by adding value. Building brand values, builds brand value. Building emotional values builds economic value. For if people believe in what they do, are committed to delivering it, and do it in a way that satisfies their customers, themselves, and the community in which they work, then the business as a whole will benefit.

If you believe valueS create valuE, then we need to link the two together by what we SAY, DO, and how we LOOK, and what we measure to demonstrate success. First, how do you talk about values and value? You use words like "important" and "we deliver" because they have much more common currency than "values" and you use the words "our" and "us" because they have the same team building power as "we."

method

What to SAY...

- "What's important to us is..."
- "What we value is..."
- "What our customers, our staff, and their suppliers say about us is that we..."
- "We deliver... on time, every time."
- "We'll make sure that..."
- "We are passionate about..."
- "We are proud to announce..."
- "We hate it when..."

These are valueS! These can deliver valuE when everyone is working to live up to their valueS; in simple terms, the things that are important to us, the things "we" care about, what makes our jobs worthwhile. It is imperative that the values are developed by a representative cross section of the organization as well as the board – otherwise the "we" will be meaningless and risk being treated with disdain by the majority. Even more important is to then turn these values into behaviors that represent these values – the SAY, DO, and LOOK that shows you live the values and turn them into value.

chef's notes

Sadly "values" in organizations are often just a list of words such as openness, honesty, integrity, customer focus, innovation, tagged on to the end of the vision. Stop publishing these. They can do more harm than good, especially if no-one believes you really care about them!

I see no value...

the secret ingredients
the hidden value in your business and brand values

Now you have the recipes for defining and creating ownership of your vision, mission, and values but how do you make sure these leadership dishes are a success? You have to have or add some "secret ingredients" – ones that create real and lasting value. These "secret ingredients" can only come from deep in people's hearts, from their desire to create wealth for your organization and/or add value to the world we live in. What are these? Our emotions.

It is our emotions and how we use them that are the hidden value that lie beneath everything you do in your business. It is our emotions that drive everything you say and help create your image, or how you look and live your brand.

The hidden value in your business and brand values come by creating the right emotional mix.

the emotional mix

- the positive emotions – the secret ingredients that work
- the negative emotions – the red hot peppers that need careful measuring
- what's in the cupboard? What sort of culture do we have?
- the shopping list – what sort of culture do we want?

the secret ingredients

If you want people to be part of a team, we have seen how important it is that they can say "we." Just watch how long it takes for a new recruit to stop saying "you" – like "why do *you* do it this way/that way/the other way" and start saying "we..." (And not "We used to do it this way in my old company!") What you want to hear is "*We* did this/that/the other – and *we* succeeded in a way that made me feel proud of what *we* do and how *we* do it."

Why do we feel part of a team? Simple, but difficult to achieve, because you have to work very, very hard to bring out the secret ingredients that make people feel good when working with others. These secret ingredients are the emotions like pride and trust that drive us as people and make us work and feel part of a team. These are part of the things we value or are important to us.

Positive emotions improve and sustain motivation and morale which in turn develops a climate, which generates the culture in which we work every day of our lives. Likewise, there are negative emotions that de-motivate, cause poor morale, absenteeism, and often create the poor quality work which many organizations have often addressed by replacing people with machines.

Up until now few organizations have really understood how to increase the assets of positive emotions within their people, never mind actually assessing their value and putting them on the books. Read on.... with feeling. See how much you and your organization use or value these "secret ingredients."

the secret ingredients revealed – discovering, managing, and measuring the positive emotions

what do you think, feel, and believe – is it hidden?

Before we start listing the positive emotions, we had better say why they are "secret" and why they are "ingredients."

- They are secret, because emotions – all those things wrapped around what we THINK, FEEL, and BELIEVE – are kept hidden until they are expressed in what you SAY, DO, and how you LOOK. For example, think how you might feel when you think "I *love* this business!" Now imagine what you might SAY, DO, and LOOK like to express this emotion. And what if you don't love the business?

- They are critical ingredients in every organization because it is emotions *not* knowledge that creates the will and desire to lead, manage, and run every organization. Why, I often ask, have we had the focus on "knowledge management"? It is emotions, which, if we managed, people would seek out, or give answers and information, not have to have them "managed" into or out of them.

Creating the list of these secret ingredients is the first stage to bringing them out into the open and recognizing we have to use them in any recipe for success. This may seem obvious, but how many organizations are not prepared to talk about or list, far less research and evaluate, how much, or how little emotion is present within the people in their organization?

Of course there are annual attitude surveys. You study the results, think they are just as bad as last time, have little idea what to do to improve them (which is why they are just as bad as last time), and then return to the "real job" of running the business. Sound familiar? It is what I have witnessed in over 25 years in business.

These "secret ingredients," our emotions, are the very stuff of business. Emotions are the basis of relationships and the backbone for delivering every form of business success. How do we make the most of them? It is in the act of listening, talking about, and measuring these emotional ingredients, witnessed in every human interaction, when you will begin to sow the seeds of a new climate. We are talking here about a new language, a language about emotions, to an area normally reserved for cold, harsh words of facts, figures, and formulae. Let's call this being "emotionally articulate" – something that organizations are not good at. Emotional intelligence is about having the ability to use your emotions, but we need to surface what these emotions are before we can use them in any recipe for business success.

So for now, let's talk about the **ten dynamic emotions** (from my book *Emotional Capital*) – that are the secret ingredients that are shaping (or not) your organization.

think feel believe

secret ingredient number 1 – obsession
a persistent idea that constantly forces its way into consciousness

The people I work with are obsessed. Not with petty issues that have no bearing or impact on the success of the business. No, they are obsessed with helping our clients achieve better business results. Obsessed with being the best in their industry and being part of a winning team. It's helped ensure our consistent growth and our businesses success.

is it hidden or visible?

Is obsession important in your business? Do you value it as a driver of the things you make and do? What kind of things are your people obsessed with? Are they obsessed with things that have a positive impact on the business, such as on-time delivery? How obsessed are you, your bosses, your colleagues, your people? How driven are they by persistent ideas that constantly force their way into the consciousness of the organization?

How often do they talk about an obsession for innovation, quality, product, service, people? Obsession is the emotion that gets most entrepreneurs out of bed every day – so if you want that level of energy, a good place to start being obsessed is with obsession itself!

chef's notes

Ask yourself: Are the people in this business obsessed? What are our people obsessed about? Is that obsession impacting our bottom line, for better or for worse? Could we tap into our people's obsessions to ensure they remain motivated and committed to the goals in hand?

obsession

secret ingredient number 2 – challenge
the desire to rise up, fight, and win, especially against the odds

When the odds are stacked against you, as they are in most businesses facing intense competition, economic cycles, natural or man-made disasters, crises, accidents, wars, and the usual ups and downs of business life in every form, how much desire is there in your people to rise up, fight, and win?

Can you score on a rating of one to ten how well your people will react when the heat in the kitchen turns into a fire? And, just as importantly, how often do you talk about the feelings caused by new challenges, be they positive, like being part of the team that proposed a new innovation, or negative like the feeling you get from a competitor beating you to market?

Does your business climate accept challenges as a natural – and positive – part of daily business? Do your people look at challenges as the opportunity to improve something and strive for perfection, or do they look at challenges as problems in disguise?

The way your people approach a challenge will impact your business's ability to perform during a downturn, crisis, and major change. That has to start at the top. If the leaders of an organization don't rise to a challenge then your people won't either. And that's about looking for solutions, not someone or something to blame.

chef's notes
Anticipate the challenges and talk about, even measure, the willingness to respond to them – that way you will be one step ahead when disaster strikes.

challenge

secret ingredient number 3 – passion
the strong affection or enthusiasm for a product, service, personality, concept, or idea

If obsession is the persistent idea that drives the conversation then it is passion that drives the delivery of that idea. How passionate do your people feel about the things you do, the things you believe, the things you say to your customers, your investors, and your community?

In my organization passion is a driving force. It's the thing that makes us strive to meet and exceed our clients' expectations.

Do your people believe you are only passionate about making money, the share price, the return on capital, and the profits? Or do they believe you are also passionate about them, about customer service, about customer satisfaction, and about your business adding value to the local, national, and global community in which you live and work?

Like the other secret ingredients how often do you talk about your passion? Is it important to you? Do you value it? How often do you show it? Do you create the climate by saying it's great to be passionate!?

chef's notes
At the end of this cookbook look out for the "yes" factor. It's a great predictor of the level of passion in any organization. You can use it to show that being passionate is the way you want to run your business.

passion

secret ingredient number 4 – commitment
the dedication or involvement with a particular action or cause

So many organizations talk about the commitment of their people that you would think this word deserves a cookbook in its own right. Yet you can't increase commitment like turning on a tap. Commitment flows when first, people believe in the action or cause, second become involved in it, and third know that their involvement creates something positive for themselves, their colleagues, their customers, and the community in which they live and work. When not at work, people are prepared to give their time freely for causes in which they believe. How much better we would all feel if we were as committed in the "cause" at work.

Too often the language of organizations is around the product; they talk about what "it" does, how "it" does it, why "it" does it, when, where, and how much. To ensure you re-focus on what customers (inside and out) get from all their hard work, dedication, and commitment, rather than what the business does to make money, add liberal doses of the word "you." For example, what you get, what we do for you and "we," as in "We try harder." Create a cause and you create commitment.

chef's notes

If you don't know how committed your people are, what will make and keep them committed, and the impact this will have on your business, ask them. By listening to the unique needs of your people and acting on these, you'll start to gain their commitment. You'll then be able to track this against whatever benchmarks or goals that are important to your business. You'll be amazed by the results.

commitment

secret ingredient number 5 – determination
an unwavering mind, firmness of purpose

In the face of so much change, with the complexity of running global businesses with infinite local needs and the ever-changing pressure for innovation and new ways of doing things, how easy is it for leaders and people in business to have an unwavering mind and a firmness of purpose? This firmness of purpose must come from leaders. Business success is increasingly about how an organization delivers, for example, against a set of values, as much as it is about what an organization provides.

You can show your determination to deliver in the new enlightened economy when you don't just have words under headings such as vision, mission, values, culture, and brand, but you DO things that show you live them. How?

By sticking to what you believe come what may.

chef's notes
Determination is another of the valueS that delivers valuE, especially when the going gets tough. Because that's when the tough get going. This is determination!

determination

secret ingredient number 6 – delight
the act of receiving pleasure like fun, laughter, amusement

Pleasure? Fun? Laughter? Amusement? But surely says the tough boss, these belong to somewhere like Disneyland? Surely says the skeptic, these belong to the world of entertainment, of theaters, cinema, circus, theme parks? Surely says the cynic, these don't belong to the world of business, of profit and loss, of share price?

Surely says the business-driven operator, you wouldn't say at an analysts meeting, "Our fun rating has reached an all-time high! And our laughter levels are off the scale."

But why not? Especially if you could say that and "These ratings have improved our sales to our customers by 100 percent, our cost to income ratio by 30 percent, our profitability by 50 percent, and our level of innovation and new product introductions by 200 percent."

What if you could also say that "As a result of our reputation as a great place to work, where it's fun to be, we're attracting the best, brightest, dedicated work force of any organization, never mind our market sector"? What if you could say that? Well, you can say it – the challenges are that you have to prove it and you have to be living it.

delight

secret ingredient number 7 – love
great affection or attachment, to want to give

"Love! In business, never!" If people in your business aren't saying "I love doing this stuff" or just "I LOVE this business" then you have probably the biggest problem of all.

I remember one of the great American sales gurus Brian Tracy (more of him later) telling the story of his meeting an old Indian woman who said as he left her, "Thank you for being with me today, I like myself when I'm with you." So if you love what you do then the chances are that, that feeling in your heart is you, enjoying being you, feeling good about what is around you.

Yet we seem to have the opposite in too many businesses – "I hate this job." Or "I hate my boss/ colleagues/this place, etc." In other words, "I don't like being with myself when I am here." Guess how long you put up with that?

> ### chef's notes
> Look for signs in your business that your people love to work there. Do people really "love" working here? This is one not so secret ingredient you can add to every recipe.

all you need is
love
love
love
love
love
love
is all you need

secret ingredient number 8 – pride
a feeling of honor and self respect, a sense of personal worth and organizational worth

Note the order in the definition – a sense of personal worth followed by organizational worth. How can you feel proud of the organization if you don't feel proud of yourself? But what if the organization doesn't think much of you? Would it surprise or shock you to know that in our buy-in benchmark survey of a representative sample of employees in large organizations, over 90 percent did NOT feel that their organization valued their views and participation (a similar result from managers and staff)? How much self respect does that generate? They feel that the organization clearly isn't even interested in them, never mind proud.

chef's notes

Pride is the secret ingredient that is not only good for motivating people, for keeping people in the business, it also creates the basis for great customer service. If you are not proud of what you do, how can you be an ambassador for the business? So how do you get pride into the organization?

First start being proud of your people. Every spoonful you put in, you'll get them to add the same or maybe more back. The secret ingredient is in what you do to show pride in them.

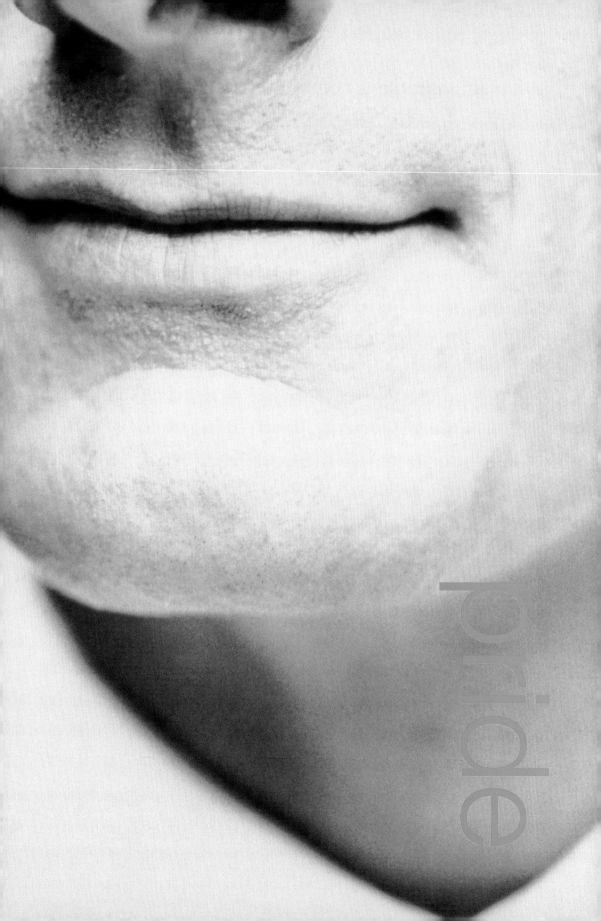

pride

secret ingredient number 9 – desire
a wish to have, own, or be

Desire. Something we all have. The desire to have "I want to have..." or be "I want to be...," is deep in us all. How do we get what we want? We have to change.

The following is an extract from what could easily be called the original "Walk the Talk" song. It demonstrates that people (orangutans and bears) realize that to achieve your desires, what you to SAY, DO, and how you LOOK has to change.

King Louis' song – Jungle Book, Disney version!

"Oh you hoo hoo, I wanna be like you hoo hoo,

I wanna walk like you, talk like you.

Be human too hoo hoooooo!"

This orangutan knows what he has to do to change – what he does, the walk, and what he says, the talk, and what he looks like to... "Be human too hoo hoo."

So whatever you want your organization to have, own or be, from world domination to being nice to customers, ie your desires, then you have to change what you SAY, DO, and LOOK like to get it. If you don't, then guess what? You won't get what you desire.

chef's notes

First, you need to work out what it is you and everyone in your organization desire – for themselves and the business – then in line with these findings, you need to work out what it is you SAY, DO, and how you LOOK differently to get what you want.

If you don't know what they want, ask. And if you can begin to meet your people's desires and needs, then you'll begin to see everything else falling into place.

desire

secret ingredient number 10 – trust
confidence in the integrity, value, or reliability of a person or entity, such as a team or organization

And so we come to one of the most critical of all emotions when it comes to dealing with other people, be they a colleague, a customer, or part of the community in which we live and work – trust. For trust creates the security for exposing our ideas, our thoughts, our hopes, our desires, and perhaps most important of all, our emotions.

So trust is pretty important! It's important as the basis for communication, as the basis for knowledge sharing, as the basis for following the leaders, and as the basis for deciding whether we as employees trust the organization with our future. But it is an effect not a cause. It is amongst other things, the result of being on the receiving end of reliability and consistency. Of being part of an organization where leaders take responsibility for what's happening, not finding scapegoats for the things they don't like.

Can we provide links between this emotion of trust and hard facts? The answer is yes. And it's an answer found in one of the most critical of all business issues – innovation. Coopers and Lybrand, in the late 1990s, conducted a survey of *The Times* 100 top companies to find out what created innovation. They expected to find correlations with, for example, the amount of revenue spent on research and development. In fact, the research showed the strongest correlation between two emotions, passion (the strong desire to create new products and services) and trust (the confidence in the integrity, value, and reliability of the people, the team, and the organization). So the question is simple – do you have trust in large quantities mixed into your organization's values system?

This, our tenth and final dynamic emotion – added to passion, trust creates the future revenue streams of every business.

For who would want the opposite, lack of trust? Who would want to be suspicious of their leaders and their colleagues. And yet too many surveys conducted by my organization and others suggest that a frightening two-thirds of people don't trust their leaders.

trust

the red hot peppers
they need careful measuring

I speak about emotions to many managers and leaders in organizations and they are sometimes appalled to hear that their organizations are ruled by fear. They are even more appalled to hear that it may be they themselves who are creating this climate of stress, anger, anxiety, or hostility. They don't think they are doing it. So where does it come from? Simple. It does comes from the leaders, managers, and everyone in the organization – it comes from what people SAY, DO, and how they LOOK. It comes often unwittingly from a language like "stretch targets," "bold goals," or simply and very knowingly "What the hell is going on. We are down this quarter and there's going to be trouble if we don't cut the costs, cut their head count, increase production, increase sales, increase market share, etc. Because if we don't, heads will roll." It doesn't take much to see how organizations can be driven by fear, stress, anxiety, hostility, and if taken too far, hatred.

So let's look at what I call the ten deadly emotions in business and produce these as a list of "red hot peppers." You now have to decide whether they exist in your organization, and if they do how much of their presence is acceptable or desirable. For example, some stress is good. We all need to be pushed. Too much is physically and mentally unhealthy. You have to decide how much of these red hot peppers you use. Add them the mix with extreme caution!

red hot pepper number 1 – fear
feeling of distress, apprehension, or alarm caused by a sense of impending danger

Is fear too strong a word? No. Whether you rely on your job and your salary for yourself alone, or your family as well, surely fear of losing your job is a strong emotion. So too we have fear of speaking up at a meeting in case you are ridiculed and indeed fear of public speaking (which many managers now have to do to gain buy-in from their colleagues and staff); this is so far up the list of things people hate doing, it is higher than fear of dying!

Worse than fear itself, as with all of these emotions, is the results that they cause. For just as positive emotions send endorphins through our bodies and create a sense of well-being and health, the negative emotions lead to the opposite, ill-health.

Fear in an organization creates an individualistic rather than a holistic culture. It can create a climate where your people are more concerned with watching their backs and playing office politics than delivering for your customers. And this *will* have a negative impact on your bottom line. I don't subscribe to the view that it's good to keep your people on their toes. I'd prefer to have their feet firmly on the ground, and work with their hearts and minds!

chef's notes

Do your words, deeds, and looks create feelings of distress, apprehension, and alarm when the figures are bad, the share prices collapsing, and you don't have the answers? Do you point the finger and look for blame?

Or do you use positive language, take positive actions to involve everyone in "digging us out of this hole!"?

Fear not! The answer lies in not being afraid to change what you SAY, DO, and how you LOOK.

fear

red hot pepper number 2 – anger
feeling of great annoyance or antagonism as a result of some real or supposed grievance

How much venting goes on in your business? How much "bad mouthing"? I've said this many times at conferences everywhere, and I'll say it again here, the MORI research figure is 20 percent of people in your business are "saboteurs" – that's one in five are destroying value. Most people agree that they have many angry and upset people who are saying things like "That will NEVER work!" or "We tried that before, I don't know why you are bothering." This is sabotage.

How much "bad blood" is spilled in meetings or via the intranet? How strong are the trade unions in your organization? How many strikes?

Now ask yourself this critical question based on what we call our "buy-in benchmark."

"How much do I listen to our people to help ensure that they feel their views and participation are valued?"

Our research shows that less than 10 percent feel that their organization does value their views and participation. That means that more than nine out of ten people do not feel that their organization values their views and participation!

Is it surprising that you feel annoyed and antagonistic when somebody else "up above" makes decisions on matters directly affecting you (usually negatively) without consultation?

It doesn't matter if any grievance they feel is real or supposed – perception is all. They will be angry if they feel "out of the loop." In psychiatrist terms their "locus of control is outside them."

chef's notes
How do you stop this? One of the best ways of ensuring you don't get anger is by ensuring you have involvement. Easy to say but what does it mean? It may mean using some or all of the menus in this book. And don't forget that most anger is self-directed, so next time you want to vent it on your people, ask yourself what you could have done differently...

Over to you!

anger

red hot pepper number 3 – apathy
lack of motivation

As I said in *Emotional Capital,* "Give me anger any day." Anger can be turned around; apathy is much worse. For who wants an organization that is dull, listless, where people do not want to work, are always looking at the clock and wishing they were anywhere else but at their desk or in their place of work. These are the visible signs, in other words the climate, of an apathetic organization.

If the people in your organization are apathetic then you'll see this translated into little or no concern for quality issues, poor scores on some of your key business metrics, quarter after quarter. It won't matter what you say. No amount of threats, pep talks or dry ice shows are going to turn an apathetic bunch of people around.

So what will? You will need to start by finding out what they are passionate about. What makes them tick and what buttons should you press? By finding this out and beginning to tap into the real issues and concerns of your people you'll begin to turn apathy into action.

chef's notes
Apathy in any organization stems from the actions of the leaders and managers. Are they apathetic as well? Or are they full of life, with a big smile on their face, ready to meet every new day with a look of excitement? For these are the actions needed to counteract apathy. Lack of motivation can only be stamped out with positive actions – what you SAY, DO, and how you LOOK.

red hot pepper number 4 – stress
mental, physical, or emotional strain or tension

Stress, or too much of it, is the inability to cope with whatever is going on at work. Once again it comes from that feeling of not being in control. The more your ability to control something moves to other people or the situation, not only will you feel more unhappy, the likelihood is your physical, as well as mental, health is likely to be affected.

How many of us in today's environment feel stressed? Yet what do we do inside organizations to reduce stress? We know for example, that we all feel swamped by so many e-mails yet the practice of sending out e-mails with multiple copies, clogging up people's in-trays is rife. Do we realize that what we do is creating stress?

We know that by attending meeting after meeting we aren't getting our work done. We know that the meetings are often badly run. We know that we are wasting our time. We know that we are given responsibilities at these meetings which are neither urgent nor important. We know we aren't getting a job done. We get stressed!

Measuring stress is one of the first actions we can take so that we recognize it is there and how much has to be done to reduce it. Second, we know very often what is causing stress, but rather than dealing with it we ignore it, like e-mails, like meetings, like too much responsibility, like the long hours, etc.

Dealing with stress happens when we deal with the climate inside organizations. Rather than ignoring the causes of stress, create actions around what we SAY and DO to limit the problem – I call it climate control and it can sure keep the heat down!

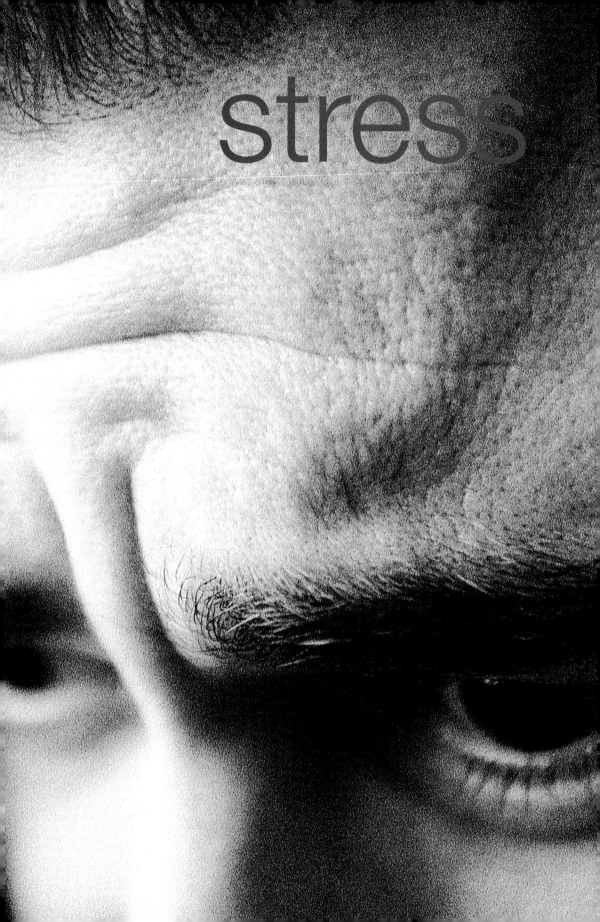

stress

red hot pepper numbers 5 to 10 – a mix of emotions
of the negative variety

By now you will have the idea that measuring whether they exist or not and by how much is the first step to solving the problem. The second step is to SAY, DO, and LOOK differently to make sure you change the climate. So here, in the hottest concoction ever, are the remaining red hot peppers:

- **red hot pepper number 5 – anxiety**
  state of uneasiness or tension caused by apprehension of a possible misfortune

- **red hot pepper number 6 – hostility**
  antagonistic or oppositional behavior

- **red hot pepper number 7 – envy**
  discontent, a begrudging feeling, or resentful admiration aroused by the possessions, achievements, or qualities of another

- **red hot pepper number 8 – greed**
  excessive desire for wealth and power

- **red hot pepper number 9 – selfishness**
  lack of consideration of others as actuated by self-interest

- **red hot pepper number 10 – hatred**
  feeling of intense dislike

Do any or all of these exist in your company? Of course they do. Are people anxious and worried about the future? Yes. Do they fight change – are they hostile? Yes. Are they envious of some people and their success? Yes. Are your people motivated by share options or just greedy to get more and more money? Yes. Are some people selfish and keep things to themselves? Yes. Do some people just hate the new owners, their boss, the other guy in the team? Yes. Of course, all of them! The question really is *how much do they exist* not do they exist, and where are they?

Over to you to talk about them, measure them, and start to say and do things differently to get rid of them. They are affecting your people, your business, and your business results. From a simple "That won't work" to open defiance. These negative emotional valueS ARE destroying valuE and your business.

even more

deadly emotions

the hidden brand value(s)
what's in your cupboard?
what's on your shopping list?

You may now have decided which of the ingredients from the secret ingredient list you would like BUT – and it is a BIG BUT, do you think you can have all of these secret ingredients operating at once, straight away? No. You are going to have to choose. More than that you will have some or many of the red hot peppers in your cultural pot as well and you may have to work hard to reduce these, before you move to introducing more of the positive emotions.

Can you imagine the leadership of your organization rushing out tomorrow with the manic look of a person brimming over with obsession, passion, trust, and love? Or fighting the evils of anger, hate, greed, envy, and fear! Sounds like something from the set of a Spielberg movie.

Yet in today's environment inside organizations where most things are complex, from the technology we use, the communication between people inside and outside the organization, and the products and services we create, the chances are we will need, and probably already have, a full set of emotions most of the time. And so it is with the ten dynamic and deadly emotions in business, for even if we don't have these out in the open, you can be sure that they are lurking around under the surface most of the time. Yet do you know what is lurking?

If you haven't listed and measured the ingredients you have got already – I call this *what's in your cupboard?* and you don't have a list of what you want for the future – I call this *what's on your shopping list?* then you are not in control. Turn over and find out more...

I have listed the ten dynamic emotions and the ten deadly emotions, and all their definitions on the following page. Cut them up so that each emotion is on a separate strip; put the 20 strips together; mix them up; then ask people to do two things to determine what they have now and what they want for the future.

what is in your cupboard? list number 1

From the 20 mixed-up ingredients, choose the top five emotions that are *currently* driving your organization and place them in order of importance. Put the one that is MOST important at the top and move the strips until you are satisfied with the order. Next write down the list under the heading "What we have NOW".

After you have completed list number 1 do list number 2.

what is on your shopping list? list number 2

From the 20 mixed-up ingredients, choose the top five emotions that you would *like to see* driving your organization and place them in order of importance. Put the one that is MOST important at the top and move the strips until you are satisfied with the order. Next write down the list under the heading "What I want for the FUTURE."

From all my research, both qualitative and quantitative amongst people and organizations from all over the world, the two lists are likely to look something like this:

what's in your cupboard?
"the emotions *currently* driving our organization"
fear, stress, anxiety, challenge, greed

what's on your shopping list?
"the emotions I would *like to see* driving our organization"
passion, trust, challenge, pride, delight

You may not be delighted with the results you get but at least the emotions are out on the table! Using these strips of card to get people to select their top five isn't just a random process. The researchers call it a conjoint analysis. It was developed to help people put things in order in a physical way rather than trying to do it mentally. So here we have a real "SAY / DO" process to check THINK, FEEL, AND BELIEVE! Have fun with it.

the red hot peppers • the hidden brand values

chef's notes

You've done your survey, you have your results. Maybe you are surprised and maybe you aren't, yet too often the two lists couldn't be more different. We have discovered one word that is usually common to both, *challenge*. When we ask people about this they tell us that challenge associated with fear, stress, anxiety, and greed has negative connotations. The challenges are those based around negative words like must, should, have to or else we're dead if we don't, etc. When challenges are based around passion, trust, pride, and delight you can imagine how the word suddenly takes on a positive meaning. This is the type of challenge associated with sport, the Olympics, winning, taking part as a member of the team, achieving your goals, being number one and everything associated with it. So if you want the positives you know what to say and do things differently. What do we DO with the results? The answer lies in tackling the behaviors that create the attitudes and emotions inside all of us. That's what this cookbook is all about.

Question 1: what's in our cupboard?

Arrange the list in top five order.

"What sort of culture do we have?" Fill in the grid opposite.

Question 2: our shopping list

Arrange the list in top five order.

"What sort of culture do we want?" Fill in the grid opposite.

- Obsession: persistant idea that constantly forces its way into consciousness.
- Challenge desire to rise up, fight, and win, especially against the odds.
- Passion: strong affection or enthusiasm for a product, service, personality, concept, or idea.
- Commitment: the dedication or involvement with a particular action or cause.
- Determination: An unwavering mind, firmness of purpose.
- Delight: the act of receiving pleasure like fun, laughter, amusement.
- Love: Great affection or attachment; to want to give.
- Pride: Feeling of honor and self respect, a sense of personel worth and organizational worth.
- Desire: wish to have, own, or be.
- Trust: confidence in the integrity, value, or reliability of a person or entity, such as a team or organization.
- Fear: feeling of distress, apprehension, or alarm caused by a sense of impending danger.
- Anger: feeling of great annoyance or antagonism as a result of some real or supposed grievance.
- Apathy: lack of motivation.
- Stress: mental, physical, or emotional strain or tension.
- Anxiety: state of uneasiness or tension caused by apprehension of a possible misfortune.
- Hostility: antagonistic or oppositional behavior.
- Envy: discontent, a begrudging feeling, or resentful admiration aroused by the possessions, achievements, or qualities of another.
- Greed: excessive desire for wealth and power.
- Selfishness: lack of consideration of others as actuated by self-interest.
- Hatred: feeling of intense dislike.

the first menu – leading into the future • the hidden brand values

cut along dotted lines to create the twenty emotional strips

our hidden business and brand values

an example

What's in our cupboard?

Our top five now   WHY?

1. *anger*   *Because people are feeling that the merger was*
                                                       badly handled and the wrong people were
                                                       kicked out.

2. *passion*   *Whatever is happening we still get a huge*
                                                       kick out of it.

What's in our cupboard?

Our top five now   WHY?

1. _____   1. _____

2. _____   2. _____

3. _____   3. _____

4. _____   4. _____

5. _____   5. _____

My shopping list

My top five – I want it to be...   WHY?

1. _____   1. _____

2. _____   2. _____

3. _____   3. _____

4. _____   4. _____

5. _____   5. _____

the red hot peppers • question 1 – what's in our cupboard?

walk the walk –
the body language of leadership

We've looked at the things you SAY and talk about when it comes to the visions, missions, and values of your organization, including all those hidden emotions both negative and positive. Now it's time to "walk the walk" and look at what you DO with that body of yours!

Tom Peters once talked of MBWA or management by wandering about. I often say that if managers upset people as they wander about – as many do – then stay in the office! Time therefore to look to what we do to make the wandering work. Time to talk "body language." "Oh no, not that crossed arm stuff," I hear you say. No. Much more simple and important than that.

An awful lot of hype and mystery surrounds the language of body language and yet everyone, everywhere has spent most of their life watching, interpreting, and responding to other people. If you want to lead the development of a motivational climate, it's your own body language you need to change. So stop worrying about reading other people's body language and start your own body doing the talking.

There are three basic ingredients; the language of the eyes, the smile, and the hands. Get these right and you will be speaking volumes.

chef's notes
What follows may seem simple – it reads as a bread and butter recipe not "lobster thermidor with a Mornay sauce" – yet what appears simple is often extremely hard to execute. No one said though that this was going to be easy. It's the simple things in life that are often the toughest to master.

body language

the language of eyes –
the look of confidence

Leadership is about confidence; confidence shows in the eyes which is why people talk about a "look of confidence." Eye-language is the simplest, fastest, and the easiest way to get people to believe what you're saying, trust (there's that word again) in what you're saying, and follow you into the future (the vision thing again!)

ingredient

the look of confidence
Eye-language is something that happens best in dialogue, not in monologue, hence the implication of the phrase "walking the talk": being seen to be getting your message across. So what can you do to make sure you do get your message across? To start off, to misquote what they say in the Houses of Parliament, the eyes have it!

method

what to DO
- Let your eyes smile. Force them to, if you have to. Practice in front of the mirror, if you have to. If your eyes are smiling, there will be a mirror image in the eyes looking back at you. Are smiling eyes important? Watch the eyes of all the great leaders, the great politicians, the great influencers.

- Look people in the eye. Seem obvious? But how often do you catch yourself looking everywhere but at the person you are talking to? Why is it hard? Because eye-contact requires concentration on that person, and that distracts you from the words you are formulating. However distracting it is for you to look at the person, it's even more distracting for the person you're talking to if you don't look at them – we've all been on the receiving end of such an exchange.

- Watch their eyes. Not just look people in the eye, watch their eyes. See what they are telling you. We will talk about NLP later and how people's eyes reveal the language that most engages them. At the very least, by looking them in the eyes they will feel you are interested in them. Whether or not you can read their minds, if you are watching their eyes, they will know that you mean what you say. And if this really does sound like teaching you to suck eggs then why do over 90 percent of people in big companies feel that their views and participation is NOT valued (MCA/MORI survey 1999). It's not just watch my lips, it's watch my eyes!

---

chef's notes
eye-language is buy-language

The eyes are the mirror of the soul. So if you want to understand people you know where to look. If you can't look someone in the eye when you're talking to them, it's time to ask yourself why.

eye...contact

the language of the smile –
the barometer of success

The language of the smile is not just what you're doing with your lips, as a smile comes over in your voice too. And does smiling produce BUSINESS results? You bet.

The evidence proves that the increase in endorphins alone brings better health. So smiling people will help reduce attrition – why should they go when they are enjoying themselves? And it will help reduce absenteeism. And it will increase productivity. All of these are measurable results that impact on the bottom line.

ingredient

a smile that says you care
A smile does say you care, but guess what? When leaders are talking they tend to concentrate not on their facial expressions but their verbal expressions. The language of the smile is even simpler than eye language, and there is only one key ingredient, it is the corners of your lips going up!

method

do you look like you are enjoying what you DO? well, smile!
We all know it takes only a few facial muscles to smile, yet in business people tend to look angry, concerned, anxious, frustrated, bored, annoyed, etc.

The language of the smile, when combined with the language of the eyes, is the most powerful ingredient in any language.

Try it in the mirror. Smile at yourself. You can't but help smile back! Try it on your colleagues, you'll get instant feedback.

chef's notes
The Henley Centre predict that work will become a leisure activity where people choose somewhere to work, and choose to stay at work because they enjoy it. Therefore having fun is going to be pretty important. Smiling is the barometer of a happy, healthy climate, which will, by my definition, predict a strong, sustainable, enjoyable culture. If you don't believe me try going round at work and be miserable – see how quickly things change, for the worse.

knock-out looks

the language of hands –
an expression of leadership

Our hands reveal a lot about us. We are told by the body language experts not to cross our arms in case we come across as closed and unreceptive. I believe though that it's not the crossed arms that sends the negative message, it's the fact that crossing your arms prevents use of your hands.

Hands are thought to be so important in communication that the UK paper the *Sunday Times* pointed out that Tony Blair, in his first meetings with George Bush, always had his hands in his pockets. It suggested he had something to hide: was he protecting himself, was he unsure that he would give something away? Now both their hands are used to slap each other on the back.

ingredients

expressive gestures...use lots of them and use them a lot

method

what to DO... move your hands a lot. try these...

- *Punch* the air with excitement!
- *Grab* hold of the opportunity with both hands, imagining it is real.
- *Push* away the problem with force, imagining it is life threatening.
- *Squeeze* the information you need out of the air.
- *Brush* away the annoyances like flies.
- *Reel* in the orders like you were catching the biggest fish – ever.
- *Clutch* your heart to express your pride and passion for the things your organization does.

chef's notes

I've got to *hand* it to you, I think you have *hold* of the idea. But will you do it? I work with many people on their presentation skills and the one thing that leaders and managers (and everyone else too) finds really tough (because they feel silly), is using their hands. Try any of the methods above in front of the mirror, or your dog. Do you feel silly? When you are "punching the air with excitement" – you just landed a huge order – do you feel you are going over the top? Yes! Trust me, I have seen very few leaders go "over the top" with excitement!

How much of the ingredient of the language of hands you use is up to you. How little you use your hands will not affect you, it will affect all those people you're leading or managing. How can they get excited if you don't. The results, good or bad, come later.

A big hand for the people who use their hands! The applause will come from the quality of the performance; a motionless performance creates an emotionless audience. The same is true of your performance as the leader, manager, or colleague.

hand signals

business and brand leadership –
from the outside looking in

We've looked at what you SAY as a leader in your organization – we called this the "talk the talk." We've looked at what you DO – we called this the "walk the walk"– and we've looked at what you do with your eyes, smile, and hands. This was about what you DO to get people on your side. Now we'll look at how you LOOK.

I call this "look the look."

First we'll look at you the person, your office, building, décor, advertising anything that people can see. Then we'll look from a psychological point of view at how people look at the world.

ingredients

the visual LOOK of you and your surroundings

Do you have "dress down Fridays," "dress down every days," dress up Christmas dinners, casual dress workshops, formal dress award ceremonies? Do you dress up the office for any festivities? Is your office in a state of distress with tired wallpaper, drab paint, old furniture? Do people huddle outside the main front door smoking? Does your receptionist wear a frown or a smile? Do you have flowers in reception – and nowhere else? Do you have fabulous coffee bars and relaxation areas? Does your canteen look like it was built in the 1930s? Does your car park have reserved places which say "I'm really important and the rest of you aren't"?

Is your external advertising a "knock out" and yet your internal communications send you to sleep? Did the recruitment campaign and wonderful interviews end the minute you moved into your cubicle?

Does your customer brand image look the same as the brand image internally? Does your CEO look great in the newspaper and look miserable as they come around once a year. Do the "dry ice" CEO roadshows, with great videos and graphics and Tina Turner blasting out "Simply the Best," really look like the managers' or supervisors' briefing the following Monday morning? Does your intranet LOOK great and get updated as fast as your internet?

Do the people in your organization LOOK like brand ambassadors for your brand? Do you LOOK happy having read this list which questions the LOOK of you and your business?

Over to you to decide if you want to do anything about this. Bear in mind that your business IS your brand and your people are your brand ambassadors. How your business and your people LOOK on the inside will eventually work its way to the outside.

chef's notes

As a person with a background in both external and internal marketing I have seen both sides of the fence, both with what the external customer sees and what the internal customer sees – in all types of organizations all over the world. Guess if there is a BIG difference! Compare both in your organization.

it's the way we do things around here

business and brand leadership –
from the inside looking out

Now we'll look at how people LOOK differently at you and what you say and do. We'll look at how different people see the world differently, very differently, and what you have to do to make sure they see things, hear things, and feel things, the way you intended. We'll take a look (a very quick look) at the wonderful world of Neuro Linguistic Programming (NLP).

ingredients

NLP studies the link between the way the mind works, how this is translated into what is said, and how different people have a tendency to say things in a certain way. I'm not going to try and give you all the recipes in NLP simply the one they call eye accessing. It's the most powerful recipe for helping you to understand the way people look at the world – and then you can use and match their language with your own words so they feel you're on their side.

method

Watch people's eyes when they're talking: they will predominantly either look up, sideways, or down.

people who look UP
They will tend to think in terms of pictures and will be able to visualize what you're talking about. They tend to talk in words that describe what they see. They will use language like this:

- "I see what you are saying." • "It looks OK to me." • "Have you got the picture?"

So, if you want to see into their minds, picture what they're saying, help them to visualize what it is you're saying – then all you have to do is to see it from their side of the fence and talk the same language they're talking.

people who look to the SIDE
They will be processing their thought patterns based on sounds.

- "I hear what you are saying." • "It sounds OK to me." • "That rings a bell to me."

Listen and make sure you are hearing them, be on their wavelength, and talking to them in a way that will sound good to them.

people who feel the need to look DOWN as they are speaking
They are in touch with the reality that comes from their senses. In NLP terms, these people are kinesthetic.

- "I feel that what you are saying is right." • "That ceremony moved me."

Base your metaphors on physical words. They will grasp what you're trying to do and have a gut reaction that tells them you are instinctively in touch with them.

> **chef's notes**
> Get the picture? See what I mean? Sound good to you? Did the earth move for you?

the wrong looks –
the poison mushrooms of leadership

You would think that people who want to be great leaders would do what common sense (and NLP also) teaches, simply study other great leaders and copy them. But, and it's another BIG BUT, they don't. So they find it hard, or it takes them longer to become great leaders, or maybe they never do. Sometimes it's the opposite, that by studying and copying others during their life from the school bully, the angry father, the grumpy grandad, they make their way in business through sheer cursedness and aggression.

So, if you want to be a great leader try not to include these poison mushrooms that I have observed in some leaders: down-turned mouths, shaking heads, drooped shoulders, pointing fingers, hard glint in the eye, knives out. (Imagine the average leader after a poor quarter!) All this accompanied with "Oh dear, oh dear, oh dear" or "Cut, cut, cut!"

Don't fool yourself that these behaviors solve a problem. These are the words and deeds of a leader who isn't taking responsibility for what's happening in their organization. These postures are prevalent in organizations with poor morale, low motivation, down-trodden people who nevertheless may, just may, deliver good results from all the "beating up" – but for how long?

BUSINESS

my "to do" list:
leadership

talk the talk: vision

1 Create a compelling statement that I am seen to have created and own as mine.

2 Use "I see..." statement to personalize the message and sign it so that my name is against it.

3 Deliver the message whenever and wherever I get the opportunity. Launch it with a fanfare and give people lots of opportunity to understand it, the implications for the company, and the implications for them.

4 Update everyone with "progress reports" on how the changes that are happening in the world, in our industry, and for our business (the "Big Picture" stuff) is matching with my personal vision.

5 Be prepared to be flexible and show how I can change when unexpected circumstances that I did not foresee have meant that my vision needs to be modified or even scrapped (it's OK to be fallible – as long as I am right more often than not!)

talk the talk: mission

1 Work with the rest of the leadership to develop a mission that people will follow, not a mission statement that no one reads! Use "We do..." to get across the pragmatic bit of what we sell/make/deliver, etc: for example we sell insurance. Use "We are..." to get across the essence of our business, our purpose on this planet, and what drives us: for example "We are a global team."

2 Check how often people use the words "We do/we are..."

3 Look for observable behaviors that demonstrate that what you say and what you do match.

4 Ask for personal feedback on how well you "Walk the talk."

5 Link pay/reward with behaviors and feedback, for example staff surveys, 360° feedback.

6 Link observable behaviors to harder business measures like top and bottom line results/ balanced scorecard, etc. It is the behaviors that drive results so hard wiring these real actions as well as hearts and minds type feedback into the business results will demonstrate you mean business.

talk the talk: values

1 Do a regular "quick stock check" (qualitative research) on what's important by asking everyone "What's important around here?"

2 Complete regular "detailed stock check" (quantitative research) with the top five emotions survey – What's in the cupboard?/What's on the shopping list?

3 Check that the important things internally are adding value outside as well as inside by speaking to customers and stakeholders like investors and the community.

walk the walk

1 Ask for feedback on how well I motivate people. Specifically ask if they think I walk the talk, and demonstrate by my words and deeds if I am practicing what we preach – especially those values like open, honest, engage in two-way dialogue, allow time for innovation, etc.

2 Count how often people smile around here and how often they smile around me.

3 Go on communication training courses at least once a year – make sure that these are not just "presentation skills."

look the look

1 Start at the front door – or even the front gate in your place of work – look everywhere, from reception, to the back door and see if everything, from dress code to color code on the walls, from flowers to frowns, adds or detracts from the external perception or definition of your business and your brand. If it ain't working for you then chances are it ain't working for others. Worse, it could be damaging your brand value as an employer and as a business.

2 Read up about this NLP stuff – better still go on a workshop. This is not quite the same as a communication skills course but can be counted as one. You may hate the jargon but if you learn one new skill that goes with you for the rest of your life it may be worth the investment.

3 Finally, give others feedback if their "poison mushroom" looks or language are affecting the climate in your business.

my "to do" list • leadership

chef's notes

At the end of each of the six menus, you now have a "to do" list. This will give you a check list and guide for the future. Have fun and enjoy the results.

the second menu –
innovating the way you innovate
when you want new, new, new to mean revenue

menu

- **the first course**
  innovating – off the wall into the balance sheet
  the shape of creativity – the squiggle

- **the side dishes**
  positive additions – how to encourage creativity and ownership of ideas from everyone
  creating pictures – how to open up limitless possibilities
  different views – how to see things from a different point of view

- **the poison mushrooms**
  no no's – how to ruin the innovation process
  no...! but...! – more about how to ruin the innovation process

- **the second course**
  a dish of circles – how to get feelings on the table

- **the side dishes**
  I love it! I hate it! – how to express those big emotions
  my top ten – how to prioritize by instinct rather than logic
  you – how to get the greatest reaction from the most powerful little word in the world

- **the poison mushrooms**
  feelings, only feelings – the main ingredients for circling

- **the third course**
  the triangle dish – how to manage who does what, when, how

- **the side dishes**
  success – how to get our goal-orientated leadership and management on board with
  your ideas

- **the poison mushrooms**
  never say never – and never say perhaps

- **the last course**
  the dessert in a box – thinking INSIDE the box is OK!

- **the side dishes**
  the four f's – how to deliver the goods

- **ready, steady, go! – walking you through the innovation process**

  my "to do" list: innovation

innovating –
off the wall into the balance sheet

The future revenue streams of every organization come from seeds of creativity that generate ideas. In short creativity equals revenue; the revenue of tomorrow. That's why creativity isn't just a "nice to have." Without it there is no business tomorrow. Creativity won't work on its own though. It has to be supported by the rest of the process of innovation – a process of innovation that allows *everyone* to transition from idea to action and beyond that into the hearts, minds, and wallets of your customers.

Creativity needs to be cultivated not just in the chosen few, in say marketing or R&D. Creativity is in all of us. But sadly it is often stifled, trodden on, left to wither and die by three simple methods – what people say, what they do, and how they look. "That won't work!" is said with a frown all too often, every time anyone puts forward their ideas. Suggestions in suggestion schemes are often left to rot as no one quite knows what to do with them.

What's the answer to capturing all these ideas and preventing demotivation? By adding the creative juices from everyone you will create the route to more than just revenue streams – you will create the route to people's pride, commitment, and a great deal of fun. The money comes later! How? By clearly charting the steps in the entire innovation process and then by ensuring that what you say, do, and how you look in each step maximizes the massive investment that companies make to generate future revenues.

Identifying the parts of the innovation process will ensure you will not miss any ingredients that make up this critical menu. Even more importantly, this way of innovating is innovative! How often do people expect you to come up with new ways of doing things using the tired process of brainstorming?

If what we SAY and DO and how we LOOK when we are doing this is not new, not exciting, not innovative, then how can we be expected to come up with things that are new, exciting, and innovative?

the second menu – innovating the way you innovate • the first course

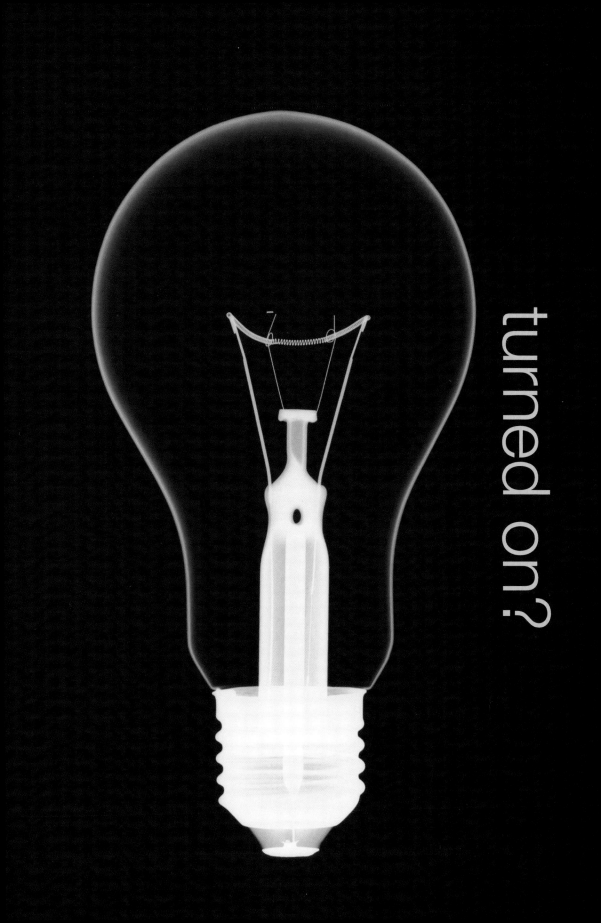

turned on?

the shape of creativity –
the squiggle

ingredients

Lots of squiggly ideas, squiggle, sessions, and squiggle thinking are here.

squiggle: the shape that best describes what you are doing during the creative part of the innovation process – going all over the place!

squiggling: the name given to that part of the innovation process we usually call creativity – to be used whenever you need to shape your thinking.

squiggle sessions: this is the time when you can let your mind and your mouth wander randomly without fear of ridicule or retribution. Squiggle sessions are best introduced as part of the climate change when you want to let everyone know that ideas are not just welcomed, they are vital to the future of the organization. Squiggling is something *everyone* is capable of doing. Indeed, everyone should be encouraged to squiggle. I have never met anyone not capable of performing this critical business process, for process it is – if only you know what to do, and what *not* to do. But more of that soon.

method

what you SAY...

When you hold a squiggle session you must label the process so that no other type of thinking is allowed to get in your way. For instance:

- "I want us to move into a squiggle session so that we can gather as many ideas as possible."
- "I'm just squiggling, so please run with me and let's only talk ideas."
- "I'm in a squiggly mood so please hear me out and add to my ideas."

To stay squiggling, each sentence must start with an "I think..." leading into an idea. For example "I think we could..." There are other ingredients we will come to in the side dishes recipes but "I think..." is the essence of squiggling. Anything else is likely to upset or even destroy the process.

what you DO...

Everyone talks about brainstorming. According to the great creative thinker Tony Buzan who invented mind maps, brainstorming is absolutely the wrong name and approach for coming up with ideas. Why? In a storm the wind is always blowing from one direction so the term implies you will get one directional thinking – often pushing you back. He says we need to brain sail, for when the wind is against you the only way to move forward is to go from side to side, just like the simple graphic design of the squiggle.

You want ideas from as wide a perspective as possible. From as many people as possible too, because it helps the process of ownership.

how it LOOKS...

You can add squiggle type props as you prepare your dish. A colorful room, posters, paint pots, squiggle T-shirts, hold the sessions in squiggly locations (we once had a wonderfully productive day boating up the Thames, one of our clients held a visioning day in a disused warehouse). You can now network these sessions and output everything in a printed book – immediately.

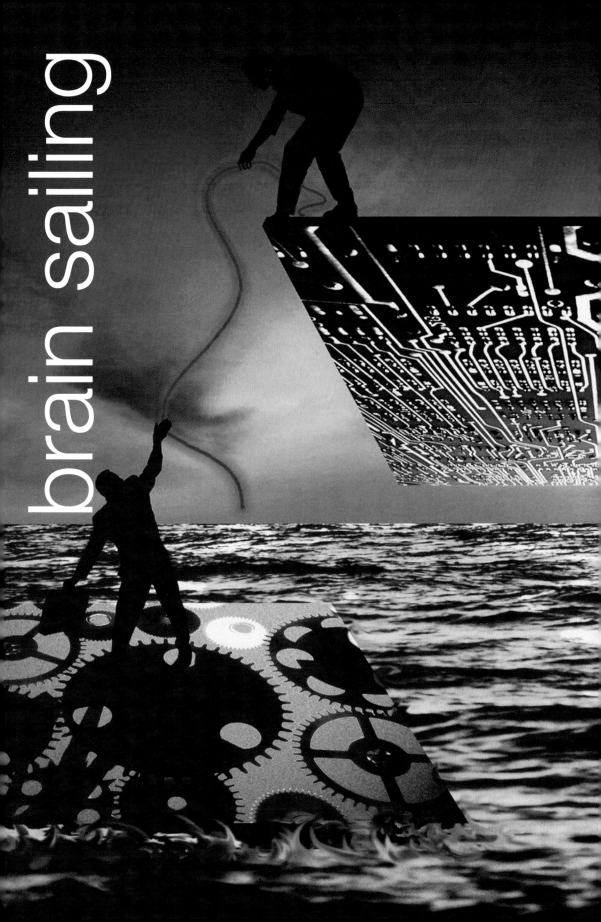

brain sailing

positive additions –
how to encourage creativity and ownership of ideas from everyone

ingredients

yes!

Yes! is a word that must be served whole. No half measures. Thrown into the conversational pot with gusto and with liberal additions of smiles, positive expletives and words of encouragement. Positive strokes are a vital part of the mix. So say "Yes!" when someone comes up with something new, *anything* new.

Why say "Yes!" even if (later) you find it is a dumb, crazy idea (in your opinion). You say "Yes!" because you are *not* judging the idea, you are saying "Well done" and "Thank you" for adding potential ingredients. You will sort out the wheat from the chaff later!

Now, someone has had a good idea, what next? It takes one person to have a good idea, however, it takes *two* or more to make it *great*. And it usually takes many more to put it into practice. So when you need to *add* to people's ideas you simple say "and…"

and...

to be added when you have additional ideas for the innovation mix. Remember it doesn't matter about the quality of idea, the baking and testing comes later; no one knows if it will or won't work, yet.

yes!... and...

are probably the two most powerful words to affect a climate of positive attitudes and supportive behaviors which in turn changes culture.

method

"Yes!... and…" Say them a lot. These words are so simple to use, so easy to introduce, and will most rapidly generate in people a sense of belief in themselves and their colleagues. Everyone also knows that when the whole team is involved in the creative and innovation process how much more they give, how much better they feel, and how much more the organization gets.

chef's notes

The antithesis of "Yes!... and…" is "No!... but…" More later about how damaging these two little words can be.

The next time someone says "I have an idea for you," remember they may be wary about your reaction, not sure if the idea will work, and are worried about failing. All you have to do is smile (or even punch the air with a high five!) no matter how ridiculous the idea, and say "Yes!" and if you can add to the idea say "...and…" The rest of the innovation process will work out if an idea will work.

yes...

and...

creating pictures –
how to open up limitless possibilities

during the creative process "imagine if..." adds ideas

'Imagine if..." can be used with any combination of "Imagine if... we tried this, we tried that, we put in this, we left out that, added this, moved that, squeezed this, pulled that, threw out this, did what they did, did the opposite of what they did."

You get the idea! Now imagine if you start to get others to "Imagine if..."

after the creative process "imagine if..." points to the potential

After the creative process "Imagine if..." helps people see the implications of the ideas, for example "Imagine if we sold this all over the world." "Imagine if we raised $10 million to launch this new dot com company." You don't have to imagine any more! This was "Imagine if..." taken to the nth degree! "Imagine if we ran an advertising campaign to launch this."

method

You can use "Imagine if..." at any time to push your ideas way beyond the limits. Try "Imagine if this could..." with a combination of ludicrous ideas like" "Imagine if it could take us to the moon instantly." "Imagine if this could turn itself off just by thinking at it." "Imagine if it could allow me to see anything I want anywhere." "Imagine if this could cure disease by just thinking about it."

As a phrase, "Imagine if..." works really well as a way of getting people to buy in to the future. "Imagine if we were working in the new factory instead of this old one." This lets the other people do the imagining rather than yourself telling them what might happen: in this way they use their own vision which they will "see, hear, feel" in their own unique way.

"Imagine if you used 'Imagine if...',," and you will be surprised at the incredible ideas and opportunities you discover!

chef's notes
We use "Imagine if..." all the time in client presentations and pitches so that our clients see for themselves what could be rather than us telling them. We won the British Airways Putting People First Again staff campaign which impacted on 60,000+ people all over the world. BA were able to "Imagine if..." the ideas and the campaign we put in was a success – and it was! A huge success. "Imagine if... you had a campaign like that for your staff."

the second menu – innovating the way you innovate • the side dishes

imagine if...

different views...
how to see things from a different point of view

ingredients

If it were...

- "a beam of light, what would happen to me?" Out popped e=mc^2.
- "a car, animal, tree, chemical, person, color, food... what would it look, taste, sound, feel like?"
- "designed by... Calvin Klein, Leonardo da Vinci, Margaret Thatcher, Mao Tse Tung, Mr Spock, a Klingon, etc... what would it look, taste, sound, feel like?"

method

Use this ingredient to step outside the box. (We will be stepping in the box later.) "If it were a..." is a useful phrase to throw in when you want to encourage different thinking or when you run out of ideas. (However, try not to sound as if you are fed up or exasperated by the lack of ideas; you could be the one holding back the group. Remember, life is a mirror. You get back what you put in. If your organization is not getting back the levels of innovation it needs/must have, then look at the climate for clues to what is stopping the development of an innovative culture.)

If it were a... what?

If you can't work our what it might be like don't despair. Help is at hand. Often we need pictures to help release the creative juices from the thought processes – use children's books, photography books, car magazines to find the subject matter, any subject matter to stimulate the thinking. Other images, like pictures of animals, are only there as props, but what props! Think of how God created giraffes when saying "If it had to reach tall trees, what would it look like?" Think of "If it were a... polar bear or bee or flower" and anything else that you can find.

> **chef's notes**
> The greatest squiggle of them all has come up with a universe the like of which man can only play at creating and improving, so use everything there is to start you off on a different track, or get you out of the box you are in. It will generate different perspectives and, at the very least, will not leave you with only slight modifications or additions to what you already have.

no no's –
how to ruin the innovation process

you are allowed no no's

You cannot say "NO!"

you are allowed NO negative feelings

"I'm not sure about this," for example, is banned.

you are allowed NO negative comments

"This is *^%*!" is also banned.

Indeed...

you are allowed no feelings or comments at all about any of the ideas. Your chance to say how you feel will come soon! See the *Circles* recipes in the next course.

Positive strokes are allowed but only for encouragement, "YES! More Ideas!" but not to pass judgment on the merit of an idea.

NO thinking about the implications like "How will we do that?" See the *Triangle* recipe later.

NO details like "XYZ has just launched one of those." See the *Box* recipe at the end of this section.

NO frowns, grimacing, yeuch looks of any description. No raised eyebrows or secret looks from one to another as if to say things like "Oh he's always coming up with awful stuff like this."

What you SAY and DO and how you LOOK in generating ideas is as important as what you THINK, FEEL, and BELIEVE.

chef's notes
You may think NO is a bad enough word BUT you would be wrong! What's next will stop you in your tracks.

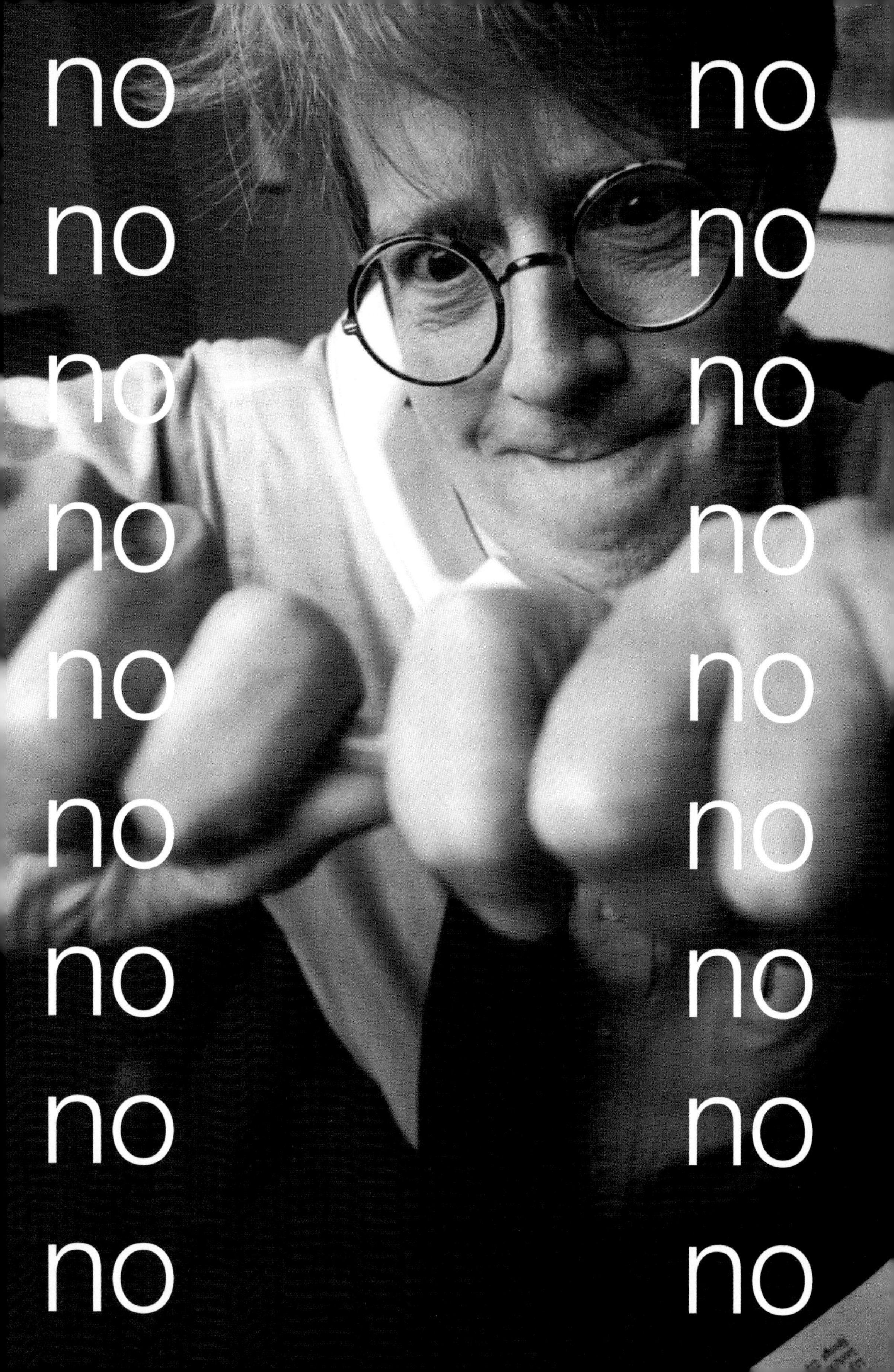
no
no
no
no
no
no
no
no
no
no
no
no
no
no
no
no
no
no

no...! but...! –
more about how to ruin the innovation process

A golden rule of great cooking: never use a poison mushroom! Pretty obvious. Yet how often do you hear poison mushroom words in business? You tell me. The worst kind is negativity.

So... when you are squiggling – especially when you are squiggling – avoid two varieties at all costs – they are lethal! The first we have already met is NO!, the other is BUT! Add them together and it's called No!... but...! The two most negative words in the English language.

These poison mushroom words demonstrate your belief that only you (or maybe marketing or R&D) are the owner of all that is good and great in the creative and innovative process. Everyone is creative. BUT... everyone knows how it feels when they are told any variation of No!; no...but..., or even yes... but..., as in these examples;

- "No, that won't work. Trust me we tried that before. It was a waste of time, money, resources, etc."
- "No, I don't like it. But you could try this idea. It always works for me."
- "Yes, it could work, but how about this instead..."

chef's notes

However... if you must say but, try saying however instead. But is a stopping word. It STOPS you – in your tracks. However is a going word. It keeps the conversation going, and your relationships too!

Try "yes, and..." just once, and you'll see the difference two little words can make.

no...

but...

a dish of circles –
how to get feelings on the table

Here's another quick definition to put more shape into the creative process.

circle

The shape that best describes what you are doing – going round and checking where people are at!

A name to give that part of the innovation process you could call "emotioning." This is the process of encouraging others to let their feelings show, to express their excitement or their worries about the ideas generated, without the need to be logical or rational. It's the people element in the process.

ingredients

circling, circle sessions
Circling is a time to respect that ingredient we call gut feel or intuition. And respect people who are revealing their instincts in a public situation, be they loud or quiet, big contributors or not. Their feelings may be right or wrong, but ignoring or, worse, riding roughshod over their concerns or enthusiasm, is going to stifle the creative process. I feel... is the essence of a circle session.

Circle sessions are best introduced as part of the climate change when you want to let everyone know that feelings are not just welcomed, they are vital to the innovation process. Ownership is encouraged, sabotage is avoided.

method

what you SAY…
When you are ready to move into circling, all you have to do is to make sure that you label the process and check that others are ready to move with you. When you have agreement, start by saying:

- "I feel..." or "How do you feel?" Easy!
- "I believe that..." can be added from the heart at any time. This goes even deeper than feelings, so listen out for the "believe" word.
- "I don't know why, I just sense that we could..." This gets out all those physical sensations we get, like when our gut is really telling us something that our head may not be.

All these ingredients allow you to take that uncertain/certain/half formed/curious tingling feeling and express it without reservation, justification, fear of retribution or derision.

chef's notes
Feelings can be even more powerful than the ideas themselves. For without the right emotions the ideas would never get off the ground. Negative emotions will kill off most ideas, so by getting them on to the table at least you know they are there, positive or negative, and you can then start to tackle them.

I love it! I hate it! –
how to express those big emotions

ingredients

Try this for opening the emotional pressure cooker...
"I don't know why but I feel that idea is great/it sucks/I love it/I hate it/I feel uneasy/I feel excited!!!"

method

Say whatever you FEEL. Say it with real expression in your voice! Add in any facial expression you like, from the wrinkled nose to a huge idiotic grin. If you really want to innovate, then you'd better feel it's worth it. And if you are really sure it won't work, say so now!

Whatever you do, if you want results from your innovation process, or any other process come to that, you had better find out not what people think, but what they FEEL. They can think it is a logical, rational, sensible thing to do – and they can still hate it!

chef's notes

People often fail to use these simple ingredients about feelings for fear of exposing themselves, for fear of being caught out disagreeing, fear of being ostracized because of different views, etc. By encouraging people to use words about how you FEEL, you start the conversational part of this cooking process. No words, no cooking!

I love it!

my top ten –
how to prioritize by instinct rather than logic

ingredients

This is the time to distil all the ideas down to a top ten list – without upsetting people (well, not too much!)

- "What's OUR Top Ten? Let's have a show of hands..."
  Use this for running a group session for prioritizing.
- "What's YOUR No1."
  Use this for involving everyone and really getting to know what excites them.
- "Let's put ticks against the ones we like – without having to say why."
  Use this for assessing all the ideas in a simple way.
- "Let's bunch all the ideas in groups to make it easy to see the patterns."
  A really easy process if you use Post-its or magnetic board strips.
- "Let's see who loves/hates something so much they would run with it/kill it if they could."

chef's notes

Don't be afraid of exposing who loves what and who hates what. It may be painful to hear that ideas (especially yours) aren't liked. However, if you don't do it now then it will be worse later, much worse – especially as you have invested time and money, not to mention the emotional commitment.

you –
how to get the greatest reaction from the most powerful little word in the world

ingredients

use the word "you" in large doses

You can add you as many times as you like because when you use the you word you are...

- showing the other person you are focussing on them

- you are not saying "I" and so not focussing on yourself

- it means you must be talking about what "they" want or what "they" get and not about the thing you are trying to tell or sell them.

method

Add "you" into every situation/conversation/piece of communication/presentation, etc not just when innovating, and see miraculous results. The "you" word is more powerful than "yes... and," and deserves a recipe on its own. It shows interest in others and if you are interested in them, then they will be as interested in YOU!

By their very nature, "people-people" add this very special ingredient at every opportunity. The method is for you to use the word you whenever you can.

You find out what people are thinking/feeling/believing/know which is critical for you moving forward on anything. And you get people on your side. The results you will find are astonishing.

I once saw the sales guru Brian Tracey (I said I love his stuff) leap onto the stage and say "I used to leap up here and say "Here I am"; now I say "There YOU are!" He had the audience in the palm of his hand from that moment on. Why? Because we knew he was concentrating on the most important person in our lives – us – not him.

chef's notes

"You" is simple to use and turns ordinary dishes into the most tantalizing of sensations for anyone on the receiving end.

- "How do you feel?"

- "What would you like to say?"

- "What are your priorities?"

- "Do you feel we should do this, that, or the other?"

- "Why, thank you for asking!"

feelings only feelings –
the main ingredients for circling

circling is a time for FEELING – not thinking

You are NOT ALLOWED TO THINK!

so...

Do not add "I think..." Only say "I feel..."

do not say...

"The facts are that..." Only say "My feelings are..."

do not say...

"I don't understand." It's not OK either.

At this stage in the creative process people tend to want to justify their ideas. THEY CAN'T.

Thinking is not allowed! You have already done the thinking up part. Now it's time to feel good, bad, or otherwise about these ideas.

AND IF EVEN ONE PERSON GOES INTO THINKING MODE THEN THE FEELINGS WILL STOP!

chef's notes
Trust your intuition. It's probably the best friend of innovation! Just don't worry why you are feeling like you are, just feel it. The why comes later.

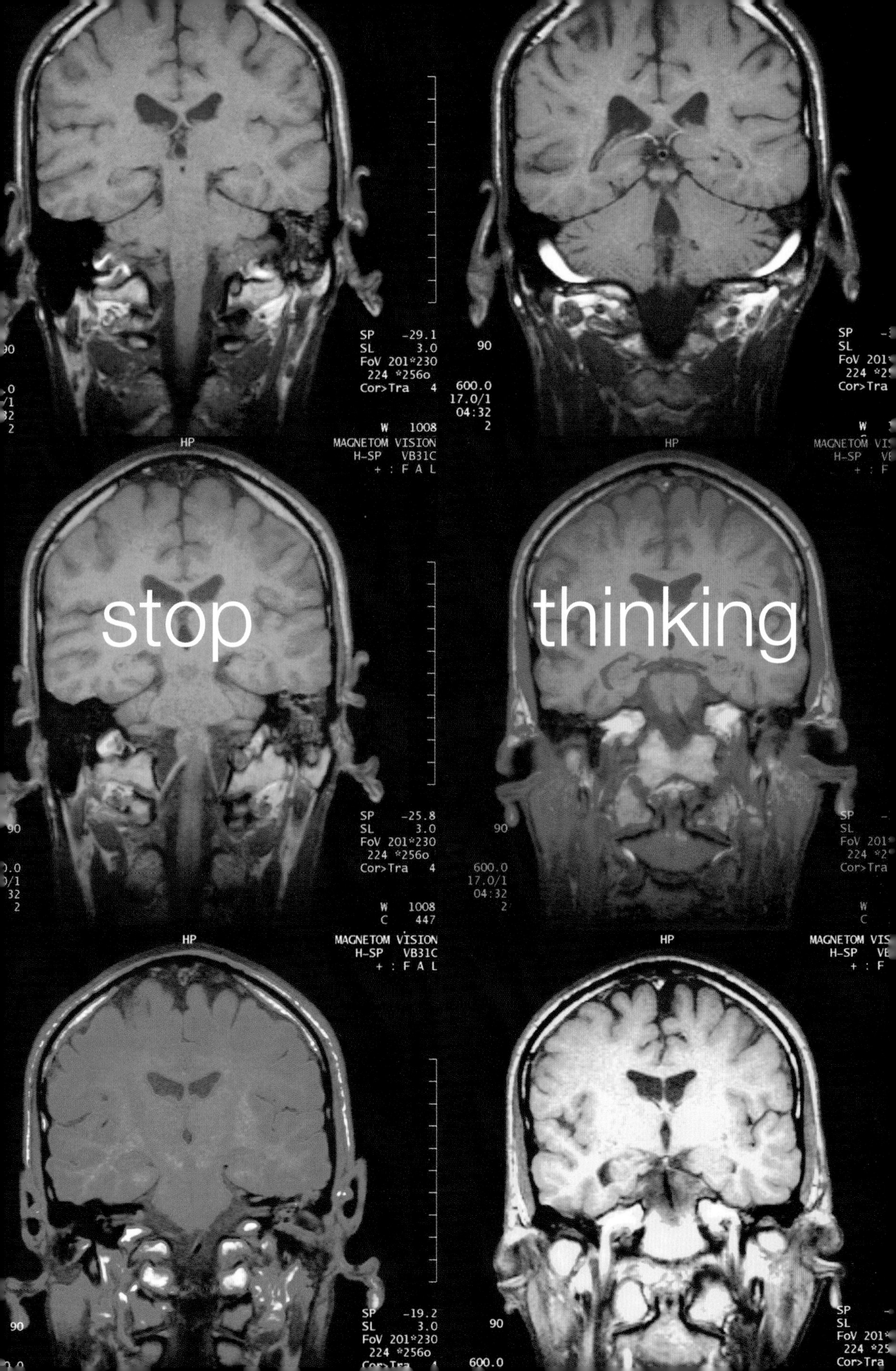
stop
thinking
SP -29.1
SL 3.0
FoV 201*230
224 *256o
Cor>Tra 4
W 1008
HP
MAGNETOM VISION
H-SP VB31C
+ : F A L
SP -25.8
SL 3.0
FoV 201*230
224 *256o
Cor>Tra 4
W 1008
C 447
SP -19.2
SL 3.0
FoV 201*230
224 *256o
600.0
17.0/1
04:32

the triangle dish –
how to manage who does what, when, how

Here is another definition for explaining why we use triangles to help shape our process of innovation:

triangle – this is part of the innovation process to inject that ingredient we call reality!

You must hold a triangle session at some time in the innovation process – or else why are you innovating? It's all about results.

ingredients

bottom line thinking
"How much will it cost, how much can we sell it for, how much will we make, who else are we competing with, what are we doing to 'kill the competition'?" In those immortal words, "Show me the money!"

triangle sessions

To be used when you need to get the buy-in of the people who tend to make it happen. They are likely to be leading or managing people, assets, resources, and often, the whole business.

You have created the ideas, found out what people feel, now it's a time to "put some numbers to all this." The acid test for a successful triangle session is to put a $ sign in front of anything that you have talked about. Second best is a percentage increase. Third best is the opportunity for promotion if this thing succeeds.

In the circle session you could/can say what you felt about all these ideas without having to justify yourself. No more. Now you must be ready to put your money, your job, your reputation where your mouth is.

> ### chef's notes
> The triangle shape also depicts the hierarchical organization structure, giving particular emphasis to the person at the top; the guy or gal who often possesses the most triangle-like tendencies. You know one or two of them yourself. They can be very nice people, charismatic, friendly, and great companions in the pub, and oh boy, can they be ruthless when they need to be.

success –
how to get your goal-orientated leadership and management on board with your ideas

ingredients

the word "success" – that's all it takes
Not success in little doses but in large dollops!

Success is a word that can be used when talking about all future business opportunities.

Use success with every idea, proposal, strategy, tactic, investment, project, and career move. Make it your recipe for success!

method

Add success into every situation/conversation/piece of communication/presentation, etc when you are looking for support from people who are themselves measured on their success rate and see miraculous results.

chef's notes
Success is an easy word to use and turns those ideas into dishes with enough spice to make most strong leaders and managers water at the mouth.

all

it takes

never say never
and never say perhaps

"Perhaps" is of no help in a triangle session and will drive goal-driven people to distraction.

"Could be" is just guessing – an anathema to a goal-driven person.

"I'm not sure…" is for wimps!

The poison mushroom of triangle sessions is indecision, self-doubt, hesitating, not knowing, guesses, or even "finger in the air."

Simply knowing your facts will be the best antidote to those who try to use the poison mushroom of waffle!

Say instead

- "The facts are…"
- "This will work because…"
- "The results will be…"
- "The goal is…."
- "We know our competitors have…"

never
again

dessert in a box –
thinking INSIDE the box is OK!

how to turn ideas into plans, procedures, and practical solutions to deliver the new product or service

A final definition of the last shape of the creative process:

the box – a shape within which you can think only of boxy stuff!

In the past we had too few ideas, so we had to train people in creativity. Today we have too many ideas so we have to train people in the "thinking and doing" processes to turn those ideas into products, services, and revenue streams of the future. Thinking inside the box is as critical as thinking outside the box.

ingredients

Box sessions is the name given to that part of the innovation process people who like the squiggle part may call dull, people who like the circle part may find interesting (if only from a people or team dynamics point of view), and people who like the triangles part love (only because it allows them to direct, not actually do, what is happening). The people who love it most are people who like the detail. They know that whenever you need new thinking you also need someone doing – and "getting on with it" is what they love.

They know you will only get results from the rest of the innovation phase if you go through the boxy bit.

method

Focus on the facts, figures, and actions. I call it "being boxy" – the phrase that best describes what you are doing when your head is down, focussed on getting things done; when the detail, the plans, the practicalities, the flow charts, the breakdowns, the tender documents, the quotes all sit in neat piles on the boxes' desks. For all of these are boxy words. These are words that detail driven people love to hear.

chef's notes

The words that you will use in the box recipes to make the boxy part really work will be very specific, very measured, very thought through. Just like Volvos, they will be very boxy! So let's try some boxy words as side dishes. Coming up next.

innovating

inside

box

the out

the four f's –
how to deliver the goods

This is really, really easy. There are only four words and they all spell detail, detail, detail.

ingredients

You can talk about ANYTHING to do with the four f's:

- facts
- figures
- formulae
- finance.

Business is run on hard measures. If you can't prove it, forget it.
These four little words may seem simplistic, but the devil is in the detail.

method

Use the four f's of boxy language whenever you need to turn ideas, feelings, and designs into the processes and procedures that turn into products, services, and revenue.

Now, if you are like me, the thought of working on this level of detail is scary. This is where you can use your knowledge of the personality types to make sure the job gets done. Ask someone who likes the boxy words of the four f's to fill in the detail behind all the things that they do and watch the look of glee on their faces! If you see this look then you know that you have someone who will finish the task, complete the job, see it through, and get it done.

chef's notes
Without the boxy finish the squiggle is finished!

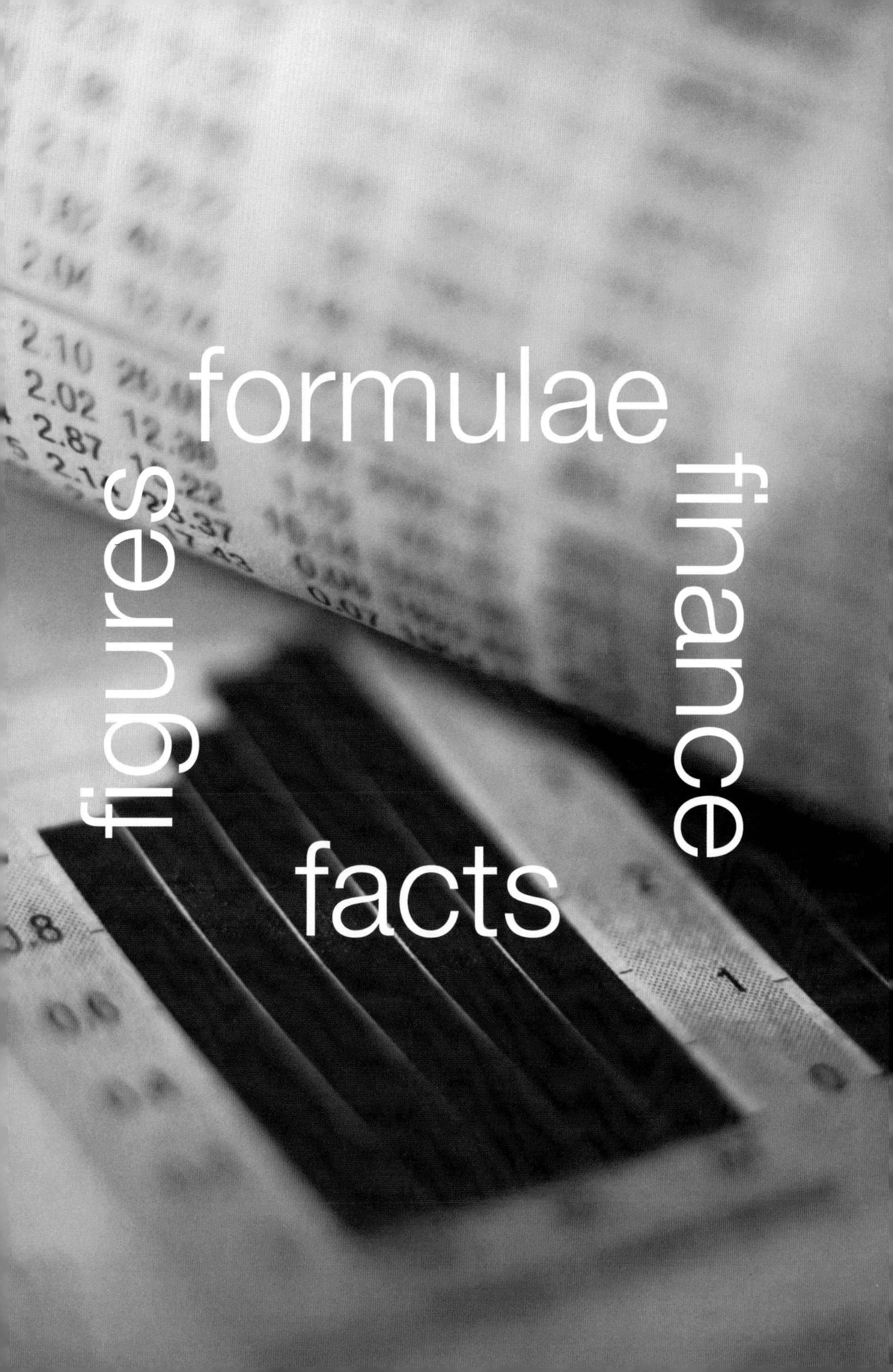
formulae
figures
finance
facts

ready, steady, go! –
walking you through the innovation process

from start to finish

put all the creative shapes together

People that like the squiggle part best may not like the word, but innovation now has a "process" that works. Following this process is what you DO. Yes... and you also have a "language" to talk about what and why you are doing what you do. Going from squiggle to box is what you SAY. Yes... and you can also prepare the room, the building you are in, and even what you wear to ensure how you LOOK has a positive impact. And away you go.

method

Here's a reminder of the whole process. This is what you SAY and DO, in order:

- **squiggle** – to generate ideas
- **circle** – to get out those positive and negative feelings
- **triangle** – to put in a dose of profit and loss driven reality
- **box** – to work out the details.

You now have a new P&L to work with to turn ideas into revenue streams. This P&L is the *Process and Language*. From squiggle to box is the process. Using the words is the language. So now you have a new way of doing and saying the right things to deliver the innovation process.

Simple? Yes. Fun? Yes. Especially if you avoid the poison mushrooms! And yet, it is also hard work. It is much easier just to waffle on whenever you have a good idea and hope that somehow it will all turn into something tangible.

chef's notes

If you want your future Profit and Loss to look good, then look to the new Process and Language you are using every minute of every day in your own organization. It's the words and the deeds that create the climate, that produces the culture, that generates the motivation and will to keep the business successful; in the good times and the bad.

the six menus for a change • the second menu – innovating the way you innovate

my "to do" list:
innovation

squiggle

1 Create a Squiggle environment that LOOKS different with more color, pictures, designs, sounds, smells! (Yes you can even get smell-creating laptops now!)

2 Be happy to show other people's wacky, new, different ideas – from all over, not just your company or even your industry.

3 Allow time to squiggle – just for the sake of it – both personal time and group time. Remember it takes one to come up with a good idea and two to make it great.

4 Count how often you say and hear "yes... and..." Compare this to the number of times you hear "no... but..." (and any of the rest of the shape of innovation in this chapter that you feel you want or the poison mushrooms you don't want).

5 Measure the number of ideas that are created and compare this to the total number you turn into product. Compare idea generation to profitability of your business.

circle

1 Encourage "gut reactions."

2 Reward strong emotions that indicate a passion for the business – even the negative ones – as long as they are not negative for the sake of it; no one likes or wants saboteurs.

3 Look for the things that motivate people to want to innovate.

4 Get everyone involved in any brain sailing, innovation is not the preserve of those high up in the hierarchy.

5 Use the word "you" more often than you use the word "I," for example "That's a great idea you came up with. You are terrific at this innovation stuff."

triangle

1 Look to create an environment where ideas are wanted, AND turning them into reality is even MORE important.

2 Let everyone know about the business issues that drive innovation such as the investments needed, the returns required on that investment, the opportunity costs of focussing on certain innovative ideas and not others. In other words, create a climate where ideas and investment are seen to go hand in hand. Too often people are not told why their suggestion scheme ideas which are not taken up are dropped for very good business reasons. This has a negative impact on the idea creator and everyone else who may come up with ideas. In other words it's OK to be in triangle mode and show the business implications of innovation.

box

1 It's not just good to be in a boxy mode it is the ONLY way to turn ideas into reality – so welcome the seemingly dull, boring detail (unless you love this part anyway).

2 Let everyone know that innovation is 90 percent perspiration and 10 percent inspiration. Over to you to get the job done!

My "to do" list • innovation

the third menu –
managing in fast companies

Way back in the dim distant past (the 1980s!) the *One Minute Manager* created a walking example of what to say and do as you go about your business so that you get the most out of people – all in one minute. This was a wonderful example of climate control rather than cultural change. It was short, sweet, and to the point. It put across in an easy to follow story that, as a parable, gave you things to say and do differently when you practiced what they preached.

Less far back (the 1990s) *Fast Company* created a new way of looking at high-performing companies with its fast paced copy, great pictures, and networking readers via its website. So with these two approaches we have the walk, the talk, and the look of managing that says the old ways of scientific management by the time and motion rulebook don't work. New rules apply.

Here are some new recipes for this millennium to manage in the "minutes" you get with people these days, at the speed you need to work and change in your "fast companies."

menu

- **the first course**
  Gtii: high-performance management – driving in fast company
  Gtii – how to get the most from people

- **the second course**
  didits and goforits – how to give people, including yourself, recognition for what's been done and goals yet to be achieved

- **the third course**
  the praise sandwich – how to say you could do better

- **the last course**
  SWOT the problem – how to find out exactly what you need to know

- **the poison mushrooms**
  don't, can't, won't, mustn't – the poison mushrooms of management

  my "to do" list – managing in fast companies

GTii: high-performance management –
driving in fast company

I know a section about cars in a cookbook is mixing metaphors but please bear with me. Just imagine you are baking a cake in the shape of a fast car. We developed the successful GTii formula for Esso over a decade ago so I am not going to change the car metaphor for a culinary parallel that easily!

In virtually every organization today the speed of change is as rapid as driving a fast car, sometimes faster. The new ways of working are coming at us at over 200 mph; the fear of wondering if we have a job hits us around every curve; we feel exhilarated when we successfully launch a new product or suffer massive lows as it fails.

But what of the drivers in our business? Are they adding to your enjoyment or making your ride a misery? Does it feel like you are in a sports car at work or is it a dull old jalopy?

The GTi versions of sports cars (the "Grand Tourer" is where they get their name) were "souped up" by adding the "i" of injection fuelling. Hence the GTi – comfortable and very fast. So here is our version of the fast business ride, with the driver that knows when to start, stop, and inject the power; the power of GTii management.

all go!

GTii –
how to get the most from people

Let's cover the whole thing first. GTii is a simple rule of thumb for handling people in a fast-moving environment. You want the best performance from them. They want you the driver to give them an enjoyable and safe journey – and get them there. Here's what is needed.

ingredients

G – giving pleasure or giving pain
T – taking pleasure or taking pain
i – immediate feedback
i – indisputable outcomes

method

If they do it right, tell them now. If they do it wrong, tell them now. How? You either give or take pleasure or pain.

- **GIVE PLEASURE** – "Have a day off!"
- **GIVE PAIN** – "Sorry, you know this is not what I asked for, please do it again as we agreed."
- **TAKE PLEASURE** – "I've had to stop the trip to Bali until you and I can sort this out."
- **TAKE PAIN** – "You have done a great job and you're overloaded – let me take that problem off you."

Is this self-explanatory? Yes. Is it simple? No. Why is it so many bosses seethe, mutter, curse under their breath, complain to others and not you? Because giving feedback is tough; even giving good feedback is tough.

G – giving pleasure or giving pain

If I am doing well, tell me. Give me pleasure by saying "Well done!" And then add to my pleasure by making it immediate, tell me now, not in my annual appraisal. Make it indisputable. Follow it up with a didit in writing (see later), an e-mail with a big circulation list, do it and say it in front of others, put it in large letters on the notice board. You get the idea. Give me pleasure. You can add an actual reward if you want but it's not always necessary, words are often enough.

The ingredient with the strongest flavor is the double ii. The first i = immediate feedback. It must be done now. The second i = indisputable outcomes. It must be crystal clear what you are going to do and it must happen. Don't say "We'll discuss this matter at your annual review." This isn't managing, it's just threatening when you are unhappy or lazy if you are happy. If feedback is the breakfast of champions then positive, immediate, indisputable feedback is the champagne breakfast of champion businesses.

OK. You can give pleasure and make it immediate and indisputable for the things I do right – what about when I get it wrong? Same thing except it's pain! And yes, pain is sometimes appropriate. Try this: "I have to say I am really unhappy with this work you have produced, specifically I would want to see..." Wouldn't a statement like that from your boss or a colleague hurt? Of course, that's the point! But it too must be immediate and indisputable. How often have you heard unhelpful vague phrases like "You just don't seem to be doing things quite right" or even worse (remember this from school) "You could do better." How? And if you need to be given real pain then it too needs to be immediate and indisputable. "I need the report on my desk with the specific issues corrected by tomorrow morning."

fast...

...forward

T – taking pleasure or taking pain

Taking pleasure or taking pain is the same as giving feedback with giving pleasure and pain but when people do something incorrectly, instead of giving pain, you take away the pleasure and when they do it right you don't give pleasure, you take away the pain. Same idea, opposite actions.

Let's try taking pleasure. If someone is not performing, then take away the things they like. It could be as simple as praise. In fact, taking away praise or indeed taking away any form of feedback or communication is very, very powerful. The cold shoulder needs to be used wisely and for a short period only. If you do use it let them know "We'll start talking again when you have completed the task." This is talking pleasure, human contact, not a grudge! Other ways of taking pleasure could be rescinding time off or not awarding a bonus. But what you take away must happen immediately and must be indisputable.

If they are doing something right, then you can take away their pain. Are they overloaded? Get someone else to do it. Are they dealing with the rough assignments? Give them some good ones. Are they delivering and others aren't? You give them even more. This is a classic problem where good performers are penalized for doing well when in fact it's time to give these folk a break.

chef's notes

GTii performance management is pretty basic stuff but so is turning a wheel and changing gear and some people are world class Formula 1 drivers and the rest of us are not. It's often being good at the basics rather than trying the sophisticated stuff that makes a BIG difference. Ask your team if you are good at giving praise or giving pain when it is needed. Do you know what they would say?

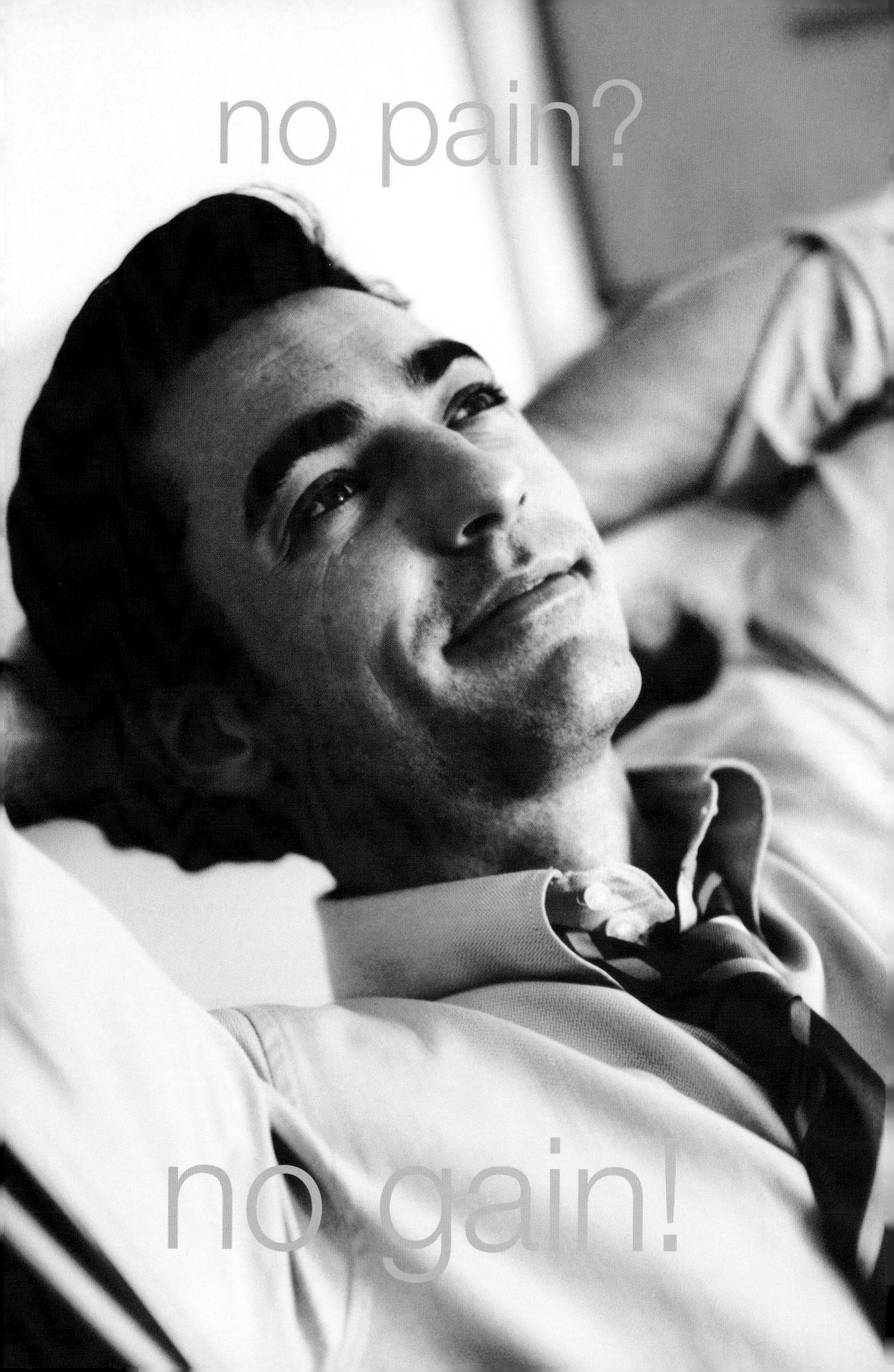
no pain?
no gain!

didits and goforits –
how to give people, including yourself, recognition for what's been done and the goals yet to be achieved

ingredients

"you did it!" – "go for it!"

Didits and goforits are about creating the time and space for giving recognition for the past and engendering motivation about the future. They can come from and to four sources:

- from yourself to yourself – "I didit"
- about yourself to others "I did it everyone!"
- from you to others "Well done you!"
- from others to you "Good on you Kevin."

So you should never go short of a "Well done – you didit!"

If didits are the applause for the well done, goforits are the challenges – from yourself to yourself, about your challenge to others, and others to you. "You can do it – goforit!" Goforits are the shouts of encouragement for the challenges, problems to be solved, goals to be hit, deadlines to be met, or even just support to get you through a tough day.

method

What to DO... If you want to develop a culture where people are eager to aim at stretch goals, then you need a climate where it is OK to say out loud "I did OK" or even better "I did great!" As well as being proud, you have to tell yourself and them that you have done well, immediately, repeatedly, sincerely – whether the success is big or small.

Didit and goforit sessions are times to get together. They are like the applause and cheers that you hear at every sporting event where great things happen and, even more importantly, where great things are tried. So yes, you can shout about "mistakes" too – the equivalent of knocking the bar off the high jump or trying something new – it is only when "mistakes are OK" that teams begin to learn, pull together and that innovations can be thought of and confidently implemented.

You may need to create opportunities for didits and goforits formally to start with, because praise, particularly self-praise, feels unnatural. Introduce them as part of a daily or weekly team meeting, when everyone is given license to pat themselves on the back. By positively encouraging expressions of success from everyone, you prevent certain individuals being labelled "bigheads." Eventually didits and goforits can be shared any time anywhere in the office!

what to SAY...

The language of didits and goforits is not hard to articulate, it's just hard to say, out loud; especially where you are not used to it. So if you need a script of words and deeds try this... "Yes! I didit!"

what to DO...

Leaping up and down and punching the air are encouraged!

> **chef's notes**
> To have an impact, didits and goforits need to be shared by everyone again and again and again and again and again and again and again and again and again and again!

the praise sandwich –
how to say you could do better

How do you give constructive criticism? Sandwich it in praise.

The three ingredients in the praise sandwich make the layers of the sandwich. There are two outer layers of praise with a middle layer of positive criticism. First, you tell them what was good, then you say what could be better, and finally you finish with something positive. Giving negative feedback is tough. The praise sandwich is the easiest way to give tough feedback, for both of you.

method

Lay down the first layer of the sandwich with something you encountered with SWOT, tell them what was good, even if it is only the fact that they tried to do the job.

- "What was good about..."
- "I'm pleased that..."
- "You did well when..."
- "I'm pleased that you tried to tackle this..."
- "I know how hard you normally work and I now you wouldn't normally do something like this..."

Now for the middle layer. This is not a "but," it is a "however..."

- "However, what you could have done better/differently/instead/as well was..."

Or, instead of telling them what could have been better you could get them to tell you and ask what they could (not should) have done. Surprisingly, people are often more critical than you would ever be.

- "What could you have done better, differently, instead?"

Now for the last layer of the praise sandwich – you add another slice of praise to let them, and you, go out feeling good.

- "So, knowing how conscientious/proud/diligent/tenacious, etc you are I am sure you will put this right/try again till you succeed/come back to me for help, etc."

SWOT the problem –
how to find out exactly what you need to know

Whenever you want to analyze something take a leaf out of the marketing recipe book – this is where the SWOT process originated – then add the right language too.

ingredients

follow the SWOT mnemonic

Let's cover the whole thing first. Let's SWOT the lot! Not just the process of investigation and questioning, but (more importantly) the language you can use. Follow the SWOT in order.

S – Strengths SAY "What's GOOD about... e.g. a product, service, company, strategy, plan, idea, competitor, concept, advert, taste, smell, look, packaging, etc?"
W – Weaknesses SAY "What could be BETTER about...?"
O – Opportunities SAY "What NEW ideas do you/others have about... that we could try?"
T – Threats SAY "What would STOP us making... a success?"

method

Whenever you do anything, whenever you have done anything, whenever you are about to do something where you have to find out more before you proceed, then it's time for a SWOT analysis. This is the time when you need to know the good, the bad, and the ugly, yet still keeping positive and motivated. What is really positive about the SWOT process is that it starts off being positive! It starts with strengths. This is a critical part of the "what you SAY and DO" in creating a constructive climate within any team, especially when you are looking to analyze problems or opportunities.

Simply saying to people "What do you think about XYZ?" will almost always generate negative comments. "This didn't work/go right/ happen." "I'm sorry/ afraid to say that..." "I know they tried BUT..." Some people just love to use "BUT..." – one of the worst poison mushrooms.

Following the SWOT process forces you to be positive first and use positive language even in the negative parts. Saying "What could be better about... XYZ?" rather than "What went wrong?" during the weaknesses section encourages people to focus on solutions rather than problems and, in turn, generates positive energy.

So, you've done the strengths and the weaknesses now it's time to make some changes to XYZ to solve the problem or build up the opportunity. "What new ideas do I/others have that we can try?" You can switch over to the innovation process here, if you need some more creative thinking on the subject.

The SWOT process finishes by serving you a dose of reality: "What would stop us making XYZ a success?" Every silver cloud has a black lining. You need to anticipate it to make sure it doesn't knock you off track. You've covered the "good and the bad" in the strengths and weaknesses; it's in the threats section that you take the time to put in the ugly!

There you have it. If you want to try it on something try a SWOT on *the company culture cookbook* – and please send me the results!

what's good

what could be better

don't, can't, won't, mustn't –
the poison mushrooms of management

So you've just heard someone's "goforit." They said "I am in goforit mode, I'm going to do xyz." How often have you heard someone else come back, with a discouraging look on their face and say "Don't... do this, that, the other; we tried it before and it didn't work." Or "You can't do that, it's not company policy." Or "You mustn't do that, it's not your job/the boss won't approve."

But there is more to it than meets the eye, or ear. What's worse than using negative language is that it behaves like a virus. Negative language begets negative language – "We know we can't/mustn't..." leads to "We won't do it/don't want to do it." Over time this brews into a hostile atmosphere. Initiative, enthusiasm, fun, excitement, and more importantly, innovation (and those future revenue streams) all dry up.

Furthermore, we may feel bad with negative language but there are other hidden psychological forces at work that can create defiance and even more ill will. Did you know we can't control our response to the "Don't" word? Why? Because of the way we are wired. According to our NLP friend Richard Bandler, the mind just can't compute the word "don't."

Try this. "Don't think of pink elephants." What did you think of? Pink elephants? So, just as children the world over are told "Don't... touch that." Guess what they do? They touch it. Why? Because the mind can only see, or picture (often vividly), the positive statement behind the negative. Not only is the action the reverse of what is desired, the feeling that results is one of negativity. In business, overuse of the "Don't" word results in a sullen culture of defiance and aggression, often besieged by trade union type interventions.

chef's notes
Just keep thinking "Future revenue streams depend on what I say, do, and how I look," then you'll soon want to stop the poison mushrooms of the "don't, can't, won't, mustn't" varieties. Dare I say "Don't use the word don't!" No. I can only say "Do use the word do."

don't say I can't

my "to do" list:
managing in fast companies

There are lots of things for you to do in this section on managing in fast companies. The most important of all is when you "give them a goal" and when they achieve that goal you "catch them doing it right." This is where goforits and didits come in. So here's a "to do." Photocopy the form opposite or make up your own. Fill in as many as you can, like the one below, and send them to as many people as you can. I can guarantee everyone likes getting sincere praise and thanks. The payback for you is they deliver more – in every way. Try it.

An example:

a
BIG
"DIDIT"

to

Jac

from

Kevin

for

reviewing the cookbook and leaving me with such a great message about it on my voicemail it cheered me up whilst hanging around waiting for a plane in Stockholm

a
BIG
"DIDIT"

to

_____

from

_____

for

_____
_____
_____
_____
_____

the fourth menu –
questioning
the art of getting feedback

- How are you doing?
- What are you thinking?
- How are you feeling?

menu

- **the first course**
  the kiplings – how to ask the right questions

- **the second course**
  so what? – how to get even more feedback

- **the last course**
  so, what about…? – how to move to the next level of influence

  My "to do" list – on questioning

What is it?

Socrates did it, sales people do it, negotiators do it (they even negotiate how many they can do!) and lawyers who do it well get paid huge amounts. And if I am not to be accused of being sexist but can be genderist (and Deborah Tannen says it too) then women do it a lot and men are pretty hopeless at it (huge generalization!)

However, managers and leaders (especially those who are so enthused by whatever they think is important) often fail to do it, sometimes at all, except to find out how great everyone thinks they/their ideas are.

Is it making statements, statements, statements?

No.

It's asking questions, questions, questions.

the kiplings –
how to ask the right questions

The Kiplings are a series of open questions to get people to really buy in to what you are saying.

ingredients

what, why, when, where, how, who
The ingredients come from Rudyard Kipling's well known poem.

I keep six honest serving men
They taught me all I knew
Their names are what and why and when
And how and where and who

method

what to say...
Ask any questions starting with "What, why, when, where, how and who...?"

What is it about questions that will make people open up? Perhaps it's flattery: you are asking them what they think and feel, not telling them what you think. Which questions could you use to find what they really think? Any of the Kiplings – but not a closed question starting with "Do you...?" or "Will you...?" You can only get yes/no answers to questions like these. Who could you use Kiplings questions on? Everyone. For, as Socrates taught us, isn't the wisest among us the one who knows we simply need to ask questions to find the answers?

Just some quick tasters of how you could use the ingredients and why they are really powerful:

- *"What* are you thinking?" A great question to get a logical answer – if they know the answer!
- *"What* do you feel about...?" This is an even better question because everyone can tell you how they feel.
- *"Why* do you think we should do it this way?" Be careful of "why?" – it forces people to dig deep and they may not want to reveal themselves. It may be better to ask other Kiplings instead.
- *"When* do you think we should proceed?" When questions will pull out a timetable or plan in seconds!
- *"Where* is this happening?" Gets to all the trouble spots, like all the best reporters.
- *"How* did/does/might this happen?" We have "how?" questions to thank for every invention the world over.
- *"Who* did that?" "Wasn't me!" "Well, who was it?" The meat and drink of police interviews the world over.

If you want a climate where people want to hear the views and feelings of others, the ideas, the best practices, the stories, and the fears and concerns then all you have to do is *increase the Kiplings*.

> ### chef's notes
> How successful will you be? How much do you want to know if this works? Write "The Kiplings" down on a card and tick the number of times you use them. Then compare the responses you get from others with your lower or higher Kipling usage rates. What do you think will happen?

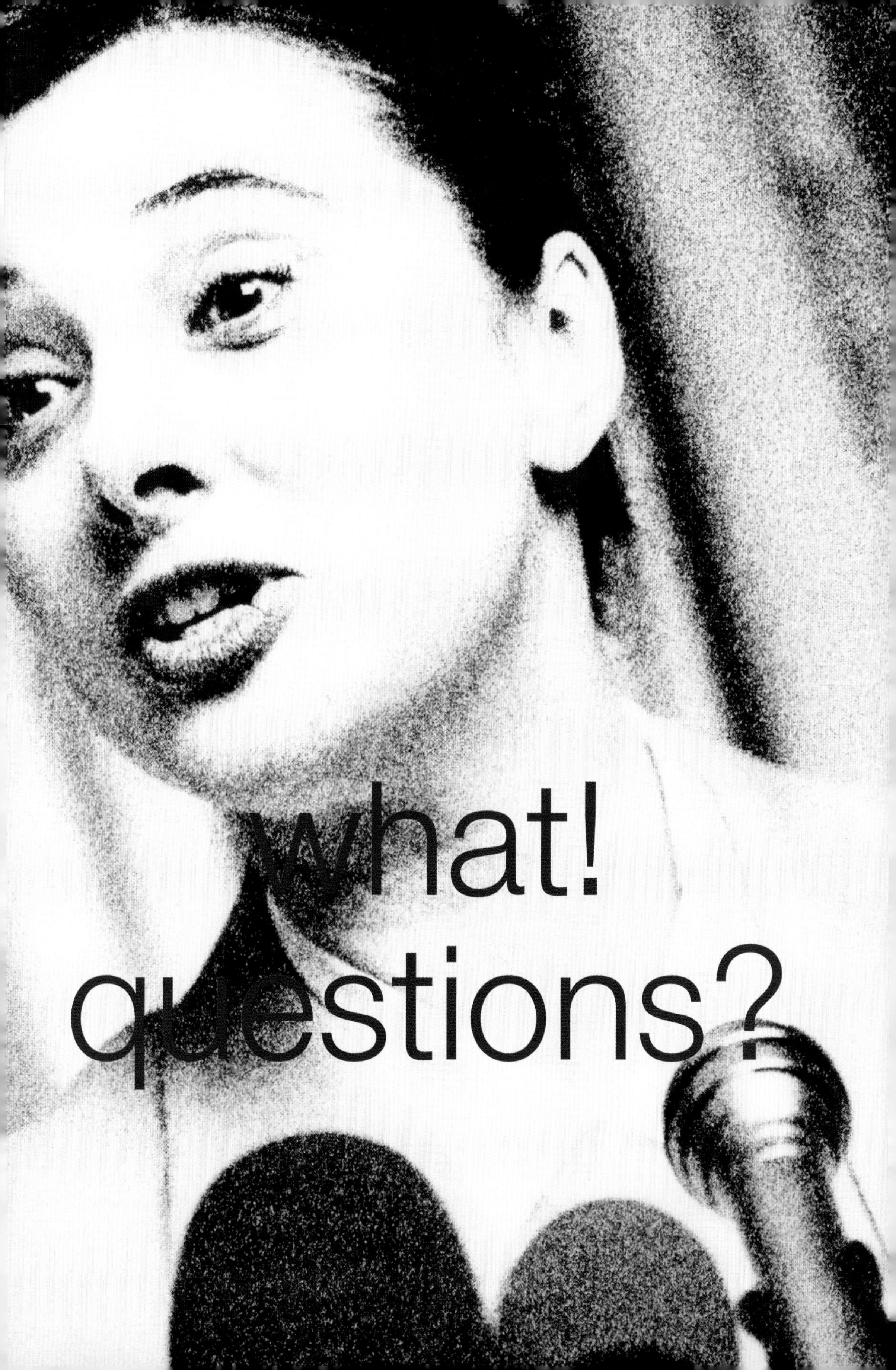
what!
questions?

so what...? –
how to get even more feedback

ingredients

questions starting with "So, what...?"

This is the easiest extension to the basic ingredient of the Kiplings. It will add more flavor, texture, and spice to any conversation than almost anything else. It moves you from questioning into influencing, by giving people ideas on which they can build. They even come in a number of flavors with pretty exotic names that allow you to reflect on their importance.

- **reflective questioning**

  "So, what could you do to...?"

- **reflective listening**

  "So, what you are saying is..."

- **reflective positioning**

  "So, what we have here is..."

method

What to SAY... try this conversation as an example:

"What do you like about the Kiplings?" you ask me.
"They are easy to remember and simple to use," I say.
"So, what could you do to ensure they become part of your vocabulary?" you ask.
"I like the idea of them on a card, and checking up on my progress. I think that after a while they would just become a part of what I say and do – ask questions," I reply.
"So, what you are saying is that they would create a new climate of getting more feedback, of 'listening to' rather than 'talking at'?"
"Yes, you're right. I hadn't thought of it like that, but that's exactly it, a new climate."

> **chef's notes**
> So, what makes "So, what...?" work so well? It's a non-threatening, simple approach with a self-effacing style. It's like saying "Please help me here, I'm trying to understand you." Try it, see if it works for you. You reap what you sow.

so what about...? –
how to move to the next level of influence

So, you've asked your questions, so you've checked understanding, so now it's time to move up to the next level of questioning by giving some suggestions of your own. I said suggestions, not commands. So, here is how to make those suggestions in a way that people are able to consider them for themselves and adopt them as their own. So, as they say: "If you want someone to own something then you let them think they thought of it themselves."

ingredients

so, what about...?

Use these words whenever you want a suggestion or recommendation to be considered:

- "So what about... this idea? What do you think?"
- "So what about if we tried Mary's suggestion?"
- "So what about doing it completely different... what might we do?"

method

what to SAY...

Say "So, what about...?" when you want ownership, teamwork, commitment, and dialogue. It's as simple as that. So, what have you learned? So, what are you going to do about it? So, what about trying it for 28 days? So, what about learning how to go beyond "so, what"? So, what about, instead of saying "Do this," or worse "You should do this," why not try "So, what about trying...?"

what to DO...

I've explained "So, what about...?" You now know what to say. So, what about trying "So what about...?" for 28 days. Why 28 days? Because to paraphrase Maxwell Maltz (the guy who invented "psycho-cybernetics"): "If you don't make it a habit, it can't become a habit."

And, if you really want something to become ingrained in your psyche (your behavior – what you say, do, and how you act) then you not only have to use something for 28 days; you have to over use it for 28 days. So, what about using "so, what about…?" over and over and over and over and over and over and over and over – for 28 days.

- "So, what about this idea, you could try it?"
- "So, what about this best practice, you might find it works?"
- "So, what about talking to Mary, she might help?"
- "So, what about getting together with the French division – they are a pretty creative lot too?"
- "So, what about using 'so, what about?' at every opportunity?"

> ### chef's notes
> "So, what about when people get really, really sick of it?" Is that what you are thinking. Yes they will. So, what about if you explain to them what you are doing and why, and ask their help in allowing you to become more inclusive, listen more, search for their input, etc? What do you think will be the outcome? So, what about giving it a try?

my 'to do' list: on questioning

the Kiplings I used

What I asked? Why I asked? When I asked? Where I asked? How I asked? Who I asked?
So what happened? So what about doing it differently? What…?

the Kiplings I used	what I asked?	why I asked?	when I asked?	where I asked?
what…?				
why…?				
when…?				
where…?				
how…?				
who…?				
so what…?				
so what about …?				

an example

when…?	when did the fall in the figures happen?	to get Sue to own the problem	not in front of the others	in the meeting room

the company culture cookbook

daily log

how many questions did I ask?

(photocopy and complete the table below for one week)

how I asked?	who I asked?	so what happened?	so what about doing it differently?	

my Kiplings daily log

how I asked?	who I asked?	so what happened?	so what about doing it differently?	
I kept calm and factual	Sue	she agreed to check the figures daily	allow more time, next time	

the fifth menu –

communicating

the art of getting buy-in

When you need to give them the WIIFM – what's in it for me.

Now we're cooking.

It's time to take the things we want to say with the "vision" thing, involve everyone in innovation, manage the business that the new ideas generates as well as use all the feedback from our questions, questions, questions. Now is the time to communicate, communicate, communicate!

menu

● **why communicate? – the science of getting buy-in**
   The one and only course is based on asking WHY?

   my "to do" list – why communicate?

WHY are we talking?

This is one of the most powerful recipes in the book.

Almost everyone knows nowadays that communication is dialogue: I try and understand your needs, you try and understand mine, and together we have a Stephen Covey type win-win situation. What everyone forgets (at some time or other, some more, some less) is that dialogue is two-way. That means talking and listening. For many people if they think they have talked, they have communicated. I call this the "corporate megaphone."

All too often corporate communication is not just one way or "top down," it is also done in the form of a militaristic type command. So, how do you change it? How do you get people to think and feel you are communicating with them? How do you win and sustain buy-in? How do you create real understanding through two-way dynamic dialogue?

You ask them WHY?

why communicate? –
the science of getting buy-in

The recipe for getting buy-in (understanding and commitment) contains three ingredients. These ingredients form the basis of a simple mnemonic based on asking yourself, and them the question WHY?

Why are you communicating if it is not for a reason? Invariably we are talking to influence others, to get them to see our point of view, to get them to do something different, to get them to say something different, to get them to look different, and act differently. We call this *buy-in* and if leaders aren't to spend all their time doing the work themselves then getting buy-in from other people is surely their job.

ingredients

W – WHAT (what you want to SAY)

H – HOOKS (what's in it for ME)

Y – YOUR AIM (what you want them to DO)

method

what to SAY...

You simply add the ingredients in sequence. Let's start with the introduction, the W – What. This is the subject matter, the "Big Picture." Whether you are talking to someone face to face, or on the phone, or writing to them, you need to tell them what you are going to tell them. Before you launch into the subject give them a maximum of three bullet points to explain what you will cover. You keep this section short and sweet so that you can concentrate on the next two ingredients. The trouble is, everyone stops here. Most communication contains lots and lots and lots of what – what I want to tell you.

But What's In It For Me? The WIIFM factor. This is the H – the Hook. This is the next step in effective communication, it's the personal benefit. Letting them know what they will get out of it ensures that people not only want to do the job but also do it with enthusiasm. The key word here is "you." The more you use the word "you," the more successful will be your communication. For example "You will learn more; you will be better trained; you will enjoy working with; you will find out how to… etc." Now you have them hooked the really important piece of any communication is to let them know what you want them to do differently.

So, finally, we come to the Y – you state Your aim. You have told them what it is about, you have told them what's in it for them, so now they're both informed and motivated, in other words you've captured hearts and minds. Now your task is to get them to want to do something different, and to achieve that, you have to let them know what you want them to do.

chef's notes

This is the hardest recipe to get right. We have had many hundreds of managers who never get to the point of including the 'Hooks' or regress after training to dishing out lots of information, the 'What', and/or throwing in lots of instructions the "Your aim."

why talk?

my "to do" list:
why communicate?

Photocopy the form opposite.

Use it **EVERY** time you want to get your message across.

Use the examples below as a guide.

Use no more than three key messages in each part of your WHY communication.

an example

---

why communicate?

Outline notes – for getting my message across.

Who am I talking with *Jean-Marie*

When *25/12/00* Time *1000am* How e-mail/face to face, etc. *Face-to-face*

Why? *to get involved*

What do I want to say?

1. *I want to talk to you about the new business plan.*

2. *Specifically I'd like to discuss our new budgets.*

3. *I want to cover the revenue and costs implications for our department and your team.*

Hooks for you – how do I turn you on?

1. *I know you want to be involved early on so I am letting you be the first to take a look at the first cut of the figures.*

2. *This will give you the chance to develop your budgeting skills.*

3. *You asked for training in this area so we can talk about that MBA you are interested in.*

Your aim. What do I want you to DO?

1. *I need your help in pinning down the forecasts on staffing and expenses.*

2. *I would like your help in preparing the forward people resource plans to meet the new budget.*

3. *I would like you and I to present these new goals to the team.*

---

why communicate?

Outline notes – for getting my message across.

Who am I talking with _____

When ___/___/___ Time _____ How e-mail/face to face, etc. _____

Why? _____

_____

What do I want to say?

1. _____

2. _____

3. _____

Hooks for you – how do I turn you on?

1. _____

2. _____

3. _____

Your aim. What do I want you to DO?

1. _____

2. _____

3. _____

My "to do" list • why communicate?

the sixth menu –
saying thank you
how to show your appreciation – with the greatest motivator of all

saying thank you

The meal is over, time to show your appreciation.

menu

- **the first course**
  merci, danke, gracias – when it's time to say thank you

- **second course**
  just a little something – how to show your thanks

- **the last course**
  more smiles – what to do when you are happy

  my "to do" list – saying merci, danke, gracias, thanks

First a story. Are you sitting comfortably? Then I will begin.

how "thank you" saved $5,000,000 and more importantly made everyone happier

Saving $5,000,000 and making people happier. Is this possible? You bet! Picture the scenario. A big financial institution wants its people in the branches to serve the customer better (that means sell more product!). It is told by the consultants that the best way to do this is to incentivize the staff. The organization starts a scheme where every time they sell more, they get more points, and more points mean prizes. And every year the prizes got bigger and bigger as people need greater motivation.

We did a survey to find out why the scheme wasn't being met with great enthusiasm and why more and more prizes had to be offered. The answers were simple. "You are asking us to 'sell, sell, sell' but nobody is really showing us how." That pointed up the need for training not motivating.

The second solution was even more enlightening to an organization spending millions on motivating: "We are getting all these prizes from somebody at head office; how come our manager never comes out of his office to say 'Well done!'? We've stopped trying, despite all the toasters and cutlery sets we can win, we just want a thank you."

So, that was what they thought and felt. What did we do? We gave the people the skills delivered by local champions who loved to sell. And we gave the local manager a "thank you" pot for flowers and small rewards for a job well done. Result – enthusiasm up, sales up, spend down by $5 million!

merci, danke, gracias –
when it's time to say thank you

ingredients

SAY... "thank you!"

It's as simple as that – and not as well used an ingredient as you might expect.

method

Use liberally, everywhere on everyone. That's it.

---

chef's notes

So, here are my thank you's:

- to my team at MCA for helping create, innovate, and inculcate the processes and language in *the company culture cookbook* with our clients

- to Kathy Whitwell, for her own dedication to "walking the talk" (she'll find out what you think, with those "So, what...?" questions every time)

- to my clients for trusting us to input our thinking into their business and encouraging me to write this cookbook

- to my IABC colleagues for letting me practice this stuff on them in conferences all over the world

- to my copy editor Megan Whittingham for her tremendous input and help (squiggle and box – imagine the scenario!)

- to my publisher Richard Stagg who said he'd goforit! when he saw the manuscript – a risky new concept, a management book based on recipes! (now that's walking the talk)

- to Dominic Softly and Nick Lakey at Shot in the Dark for their design skills

- and last but not least to YOU, for reading this book and giving me the pleasure of giving you some food for thought!

And most of all to my dog Chip – it was when walking him that I did much of my conceptual thinking, planning, and mental editing throughout the development and writing of this cookbook. And if there are bits that maybe just maybe will help you change yourself or your business then thank my parents (in loving memory to my mum): they were why I am here.

thanks Chip!

just a little something –
how to show your thanks

ingredients

A bunch of flowers, a handshake, a card, a note, a plaque on the wall, a badge, a drink in the bar, a trip to somewhere or other, a day off... over to you to come up with your own endless list.

DOING something to show your thanks is part of Gtii management and shows you mean it.

method

Demonstrate your thanks visually, verbally, in your actions, deeds; everywhere on everyone. Over to you.

chef's notes

When we worked to save that $5 million I talked about in the introduction, we transferred a small amount of the pot to local leaders and managers to come up with their own "Thank You Fund." The managers and staff loved it. We have one in our business where anyone can use the fund to buy anyone, anything to say thank you – flowers are a favorite. No one abuses it. Remember it's not just what you SAY, it's also what you DO that changes the climate that changes the culture.

it's my pleasure

more smiles –
what you do when you are happy

show how happy you are

When someone does something great, this is what you DO to show how happy you are.

ingredients

Time for a spot of repetition. For if you want to really get your message across you need to repeat yourself – sometimes ad nauseum! As marketing people have understood, you need to see things like adverts at least six times (it's called OTS, Opportunities To See) just to impinge on people's consciousness. So here is another OTS on what you do with your lips. Make them smile. It's almost as simple as that – almost. Because smiles create something magical, as well as great feelings they also make you feel great too.

method

Use your five facial muscles that lift the edges of the eyes, curl the lips towards heaven, and transform your face into something that changes you and those around you.

smiles and smiles and smiles

my "to do" list:
saying merci, danke, gracias, thanks

Photocopy the form opposite. Or make up your own. Fill in as many as you can, like the one below, and send them to as many people as you can. I can guarantee everyone likes getting sincere praise and thanks. The payback for you is they deliver more – in every way.

Try it. And if it works - please send me an e-mail and say…

many thanks

NK YOU *MERCI* DANKE **GRACIAS** THANK YOU *MERCI* DANKE **GRA**
:IAS DANKE **THANK YOU** *MERCI***GRACIAS** DANKE **THANK YOU** *ME*
KE **THANK YOU** *MERCI* **GRACIAS** DANKE **GRACIAS** DANKE THANK
:IAS DANKE **THANK YOU** *MERCI***GRACIAS** DANKE **THANK YOU** *ME*
KE *MERCI* **GRACIAS** DANKE **GRACIAS** DANKE **THANK YOU GRACIA**
KE **THANK YOU** *MERCI***GRACIAS** DANKE **THANK YOU** *MERCI*DANK
NK YOU *MERCI* **GRACIAS** DANKE **GRACIAS** DANKE **THANK YOU** *M.*

to

Sharron

from

Kevin

for

all your help with turning the cookbook from a vision into a reality

many thanks

YOU *MERCI* DANKE **GRACIAS** THANK YOU *MERCI* DANKE **GRAC**
S DANKE THANK YOU *MERCI***GRACIAS** DANKE THANK YOU *ME*
THANK YOU *MERCI* **GRACIAS** DANKE **GRACIAS** DANKE THANK
S DANKE THANK YOU *MERCI***GRACIAS** DANKE THANK YOU *ME*
MERCI **GRACIAS** DANKE **GRACIAS** DANKE THANK YOU **GRACIA**
THANK YOU *MERCI***GRACIAS** DANKE THANK YOU *MERCI*DANK
YOU *MERCI* **GRACIAS** DANKE **GRACIAS** DANKE THANK YOU *ME*

to

———

from

———

for

_____

_____

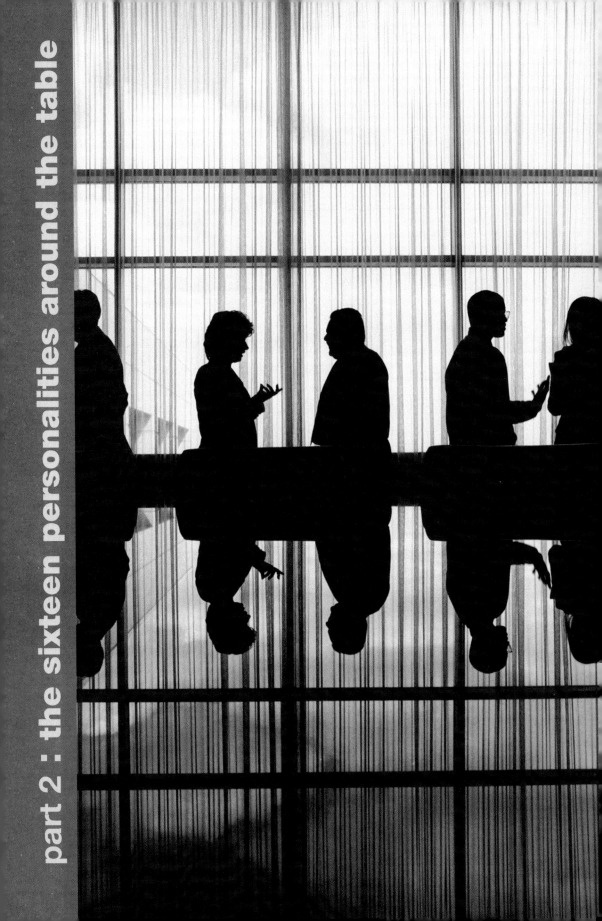

part 2 : the sixteen personalities around the table

guess who's coming to the meeting...

the personalities around the table

- **what are they like?**
  Find out with "shapes and shades."
  "Shapes and shades" is the fastest psychometric test in the world; it's fun, simple, easy, and user-friendly. This is the ultimate "how to." How to find out what makes people (including you) tick. Discover a new language and use it to communicate effectively with anyone at work according to their preferred style, not yours!

- **the personality pairs**
  The four pairs of ingredients that make up YOU.

- **the personality planner**
  The quick reference grid for working out your team types.

- **the personalities around the table**
  What are they like? How to find the right mix.
  The eight different "shapes and shade" traits create 16 different personality types.
  What are they like to be with? Find out later in this part.

personality pairs

you have been creative with shapes, now let's put a shape to your creativity

how to see if you are a squiggling innovator

We talked in the innovation menu about different types of language and processes: squiggle, circle, triangle, and box. Not only are the shapes useful for describing what you DO, they are great for describing what you are like.

"Shapes and shades" builds on work by Carl Jung and Isobel Briggs Myers by combining both the use of what I call color and geometric psychology. The personality pairs coming up soon show you how to describe your work style – your preferred way of doing things – and your approach to life – for example, are you outgoing or are you inward focussed, and are you a last minute sort or do you plan way ahead?

You will discover:

1 What work you prefer and what you hate – and how you work with others.

2 How you do what you do – and how it fits in with others.

3 How you communicate with others – and how they need to communicate with you.

4 What motivates you – and how you motivate others.

Organizations use many different pyschometric tests for a variety of reasons: job assessment, team working, and sometimes to help people understand how they themselves and others relate and communicate. Every time an organization uses one of these tests (whether they like it or not, or even realize it or not) they can affect the climate with the language that the "test" is based on. As it is often only senior management who have an opportunity to do such tests, the language becomes exclusive, thus alienating everyone else in the organization.

The language of squiggles and boxes is definitely not just for the select privileged few; "shapes and shades" is for everyone!

me...creative?

shapes and shades at work
the ingredients that make up you

There are four pairs of ingredients under the ABCD labels. I call these the personality pairs. You can only choose one ingredient from these four pairs of ingredients. The resulting four ingredients make up the dish called *you*.

what do you choose?

Choose the shapes and the shades that best describe what you are like as a person. For example, are you a yellow or a violet person? This doesn't mean which color you prefer but which color are you. You may not know why you choose a shape or shade to describe your personality but that's the fun of it! If you want to change it later when you find out what they mean, then you can. Beware though, your initial selection of a shape or shade is often the best.

If you really aren't sure about what you are like, ask someone who knows you. "Am I a squiggle or a box?" you say. "I've no idea what it means, but you are definitely a squiggle!" they might reply.

So, ask yourself these questions, then tick the appropriate color and symbol.

A Are you a yellow person or are you a violet person?
B Are you a squiggle or a box?
C Are you a triangle or a circle?
D Are you a red person or are you a blue person?

the personality pairs

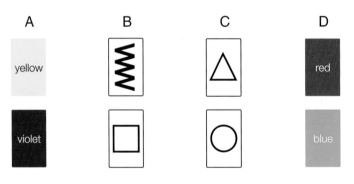

A	B	C	D
yellow			red
violet			blue

---

chef's notes
Did you choose? Was it easy? What they mean is coming up next. And remember, if you think you are not the shape or shade you chose once you have read the descriptions, don't worry. This is a really flexible approach. Just change your shape or shade to fit the description that you think suits you best (having checked with other people first that the description really fits).

personality pair A
inside or out?

yellow

Someone who gets their energy externally. They love being with other people, either to tell them what they think or to find out their views. They thrive on being recognized, having their say, giving their opinion, discussing with others whatever it is they want to discuss. Carl Jung, the grandfather of the Myers Briggs Type Indicator, called these people *extroverts*. He didn't mean they are the life and soul of the party. He meant they were externally rather than internally driven.

violet

Internally driven people (not shy necessarily) are those who get their energy from within. They don't have to rush out and find someone to talk to, they are happy with their own company. They sometimes get called shrinking violets if they take their introversion too far and won't or just don't talk with others. As about 60 percent of people are yellow it means the violets are in the minority and may be quiet around others, so they don't/won't stand out.

personality pair B
ideas or information?

Someone whose core personality is based on coming up with ideas. Someone who you can add to the team to get the creative process going quickly. However, squiggles, as people, are best used sparingly. Too many ideas from one person can become intimidating and from a squiggle's point of view, it is frustrating if all of their ideas are not used!

This is the shape that best describes those people whose head is down, focussed on getting things done, when the detail, the plans, the practicalities, the flow charts, the quotes all sit in neat piles on the box's desk. These are words that boxes love to hear. If you use them with a box they will nod and smile, the sure way to test if someone really is that completer finisher that the psychometric profiles tell us about. (Say "detail" to a squiggle and watch them run.) Talking of smiling, does the thought of tidying your desk, house, or room before you go out make you smile or scream?

Find out next if you are triangle or circle.

personality pair C
facts or feelings

Triangles are usually goal driven people. If you want to make triangle people tingle, say any combination of "Profit... Cost cuts... Sales increase... Return on capital... " They are always interested in success. Their core personality is based on getting where they want to go and their decisions are based on logical thought.

Now here is a shape that is really easy to describe. Someone whose core personality is based on caring about what others think, feel, and believe about themselves. Circles are people people. Circles bring out the best in others. They will always focus on you and your needs, unlike triangles, who will focus on me and my needs.

personality pair D
play or plan?

red

Do you like to play or do you like to plan? This is the question that will sort out the reds from the blues. The red people love to play. They will leave things to the last minute. They will only tidy the desk/house/room when they absolutely have to. Red people will refuse to be tied into things that don't leave a way out. As plans usually have to be stuck to, planning is often a no-no. They will be driven by emotion, for red is the color of love as well as anger. They won't be driven by the cool, clear decision-making process that says "organize it – or else!" That is for blue people.

blue

Do you like to plan or do you like to play? Sure you love to play after you have done all you planned to do or even when playing is part of the plan! Planning then playing is the key difference that will sort out the blues from the reds. For the blue people love to plan. They will never leave things to the last minute. What will their planning, organization, and decision making be based on? Easy, if they are triangles they will base things on "logic" (theirs!) and if they are circles they will base their decisions on "values" (theirs too!).

chef's notes

Now you have chosen from your personality pairs, what do you DO and SAY differently?

The "shapes and shades" character complementer in the next section gives you the 16 core types of personality that make up the basis for any group of personalities. It will show you what each type is like, the language they use, and indicates how you can match each style with your language so you can show them that you know where you are coming from. So, no more guessing about the mix needed for any team! Be it for social reasons or work, as guests or in teams, you can select people who complement each other for the purpose in hand.

But first let's get a list of who's who and who's what by filling out the "personality planner."

the personality planner
at work

who fits best where and with whom

The "shapes and shades personality planner" is a quick reference grid (not to be taken too seriously) for working out, for any team, who is what personality type. You will also discover how many of the eight traits you have in total in the team. From there, you'll have the questions to ask about how to maximize the strengths of the individuals and the team. The "personality planner" is not to be used for saying things like "I need a Box for this job," as everyone and anyone may be capable of doing a particular job – it is there as a guide to what happens when different people get together.

using the personality planner

The "personality planner" on the opposite page can be used in a number of ways:

- to demonstrate individual team member style – both internally and with others
- to show team strengths and weaknesses – therefore the potential overdone strengths and gaps that might need to be filled
- to highlight communication styles needed at individual and team level and with others outside the team
- to help individuals and the team see how they can develop
- to show newcomers (or anyone else coming in to a real or virtual team) where they fit in
- to create a non-threatening and fun language for resolving lots of people, communication, style, or approach issues.

shapes and shades at work
the personality planner

team name:

the people	the personality traits								the characters boss, loose cannon, etc.
	yellow	violet	≶	▢	△	○	red	blue	
total									

my notes

the six personalities around the table • the personality planner

the marketing team from GlobalBusiness Inc.

The (fictitious) example opposite is the marketing team from GlobalBusiness Inc.

Answer the following questions – the "character complementer" (next) may help:

- What are the team's strengths ("what's good") and weaknesses ("what could be better")?
- What might you expect members would be like working together:
  - (a) as a team
  - (b) as individuals?

- Who could work well together? Who might clash?
- What is the team's overall style? How will this affect its decisions and actions?
- What might you expect the team would be like working together with other departments?

fill in their character types

As you read the next section fill in their character types from the "character complementer."
You can do this with your own team too. Watch the dynamics build as you get to understand
its traits.

> #### chef's notes
> Make your own notes under "my notes" about what you would need to do with a team like this.

shapes and shades
the personality planner

team name: *the marketing team from GlobalBusiness Inc.*

the people	the personality traits								the characters boss, loose cannon, etc.
	yellow	violet	≋	□	△	○	red	blue	
Joshua	✔			✔		✔	✔		
Tamara	✔		✔		✔		✔		
Marc	✔			✔		✔		✔	
Leo	✔		✔		✔		✔		
Janet		✔	✔			✔	✔		
Francoise	✔		✔			✔	✔		
Li	✔		✔		✔		✔		
Katrina	✔		✔		✔			✔	
Javier		✔		✔		✔	✔		
Raphael	✔		✔		✔		✔		
Dejan		✔	✔			✔	✔		
Anne-marie	✔			✔	✔		✔		
total	9	3	8	4	6	6	10	2	

my notes

_____

_____

_____

_____

_____

_____

the six personalities around the table • the personality planner completed

the character complementer

how to find the right mix of people

These 16 personality types are people that you will meet in every walk of life. How do you spot them? How do you communicate with them? How do you relate to them? How do you work with them? How do you get the most out of them?

Oh, and one unknown personality.

There's always one – isn't there?

the boss
I know exactly what I want and how to get it,
– and I'll let you know it too!

the shapes and shades of their personality

yellow, squiggle, triangle, blue

Their yellow makes them outgoing. Their squiggle means they can see the "Big Picture" and the possibilities that will let them get there. Their triangle makes them logical and able to make quick decisions on the facts (as they see them!). Their blue makes them organized and very good at organizing everyone around them!

what are they like?

how do they act and what turns them on?

This is a powerful combination. These people want to get somewhere in life so they'll go for it when they have to! They will organize others to deliver the goods, reach the goals, beat the competition. Give them a platform and they will use it to give that "town hall" meeting. With their ability to internalize their thinking around the many issues they can handle – as squiggles – they will be good company and talk about lots of topics. But with their blue approach they will probably have organized their thoughts and decided exactly what they think on any topic before discussion begins.

chef's notes

I've had feedback. From "the boss" – a group chief executive who read this section and says that I should add a *chef's note* to highlight to others how to deal with "the boss." The answer may be to agree with them and do what they say – hence I have included this chef's note! However, more and more bosses today don't (thankfully) want this. They want others to give them answers – so that's what you tell them you have got. And they want success – a great ingredient we have already come across. What does your boss want? Bear in mind that bosses come in every shape and size so why not go and ask them – they will all appreciate your interest. Could be a raise in it for you too!

the boss

the loose cannon!

I love new ideas, new concepts, new ways of doing things, and talking about them with anyone interested. I'm not too sure of getting involved in the detail and the delivery though!

the shapes and shades of their personality

yellow, squiggle, triangle, red

Their yellow makes them outgoing. Their squiggle means they can see the "Big Picture" and the options that will help them get there. Their triangle makes them good thinkers and whilst they may not appear logical, it is their speed of thought from one side of the issue to the other that makes them seem all over the place (squiggling). They can be very logical (sometimes!). Their red makes them playful – usually around new ideas.

what are they like?

how do they act and what turns them on?

"Loose cannon" types are hard to keep up with. They can be firing off in every direction, often at the same time. They are fun to be with though (for a short period of time). They will be difficult to argue with as they can squiggle from one place to another with the greatest of ease, and somehow make it all seem logical (at least, they think so). They are great at the "Big Picture" and can see connections others can't spot.

> ### chef's notes
> Like all squiggles their world is full of possibilities, and with their red side wanting to spend all their time playing with these ideas, and their yellow side wanting to go out and talk to people about their ideas, you could imagine them as great inventors or solution generators. They are most definitely not implementors. When it comes to getting things done they either leave it to someone else or go quiet on you. Their violet side comes out and they may go off on their own to do whatever it is they have to do.

the loose

cannon!

the thinker

I just love digging and delving into ideas, solving complex issues, and formulating solutions – especially ideas, issues, and formulas that need deep thought – which means no extraneous people around me!

the shapes and shades of their personality

violet, squiggle, triangle, red

The white-coated rocket scientist comes to mind! Their violet trait creates their inward focus. Their squiggle, being the trait that comes out as their external driver, means the thinker will discuss ideas and possibilities (mainly with their peers). Their triangle will ensure that their focus will be logical, hard headed and clearly focussed. They may have little regard for the moral implications – they "know" others will worry about that.

what are they like?

how do they act and what turns them on?

Who knows what Einstein was in his "shapes and shades," but surely he was squiggling when he went riding on a beam of light! Surely his chaotic dress sense and last-minute appearance means he was red. How can you be involved in nuclear physics, and especially nuclear bombs, unless you are a logical triangle? And was he the life and soul of the party? I doubt it.

So here we have the thinker. Here is the classic mad scientist driven by what happens internally, rather than working in a team, be it from their dreams, own ideas, way of questioning, etc.

I am not saying all thinkers are like Einstein but this gives you a good picture of the person who loves to play with theories, like children play with toys. They may be deadly dull in much of what else they do. I said maybe – if you are a thinker type you could also be really, really interesting – but as few people will get to know you, their perception will be of someone who doesn't or won't talk. So QED, to them, you must be dull! And that again is the danger for violet people. Unless they speak up, others will make assumptions like: "They never have much to say," or "Good sort is our thinker but pretty dry."

chef's notes

If you are a thinker and you want your voice to be heard then speak up. If not, and you are happy with being seen as quiet at best and dull at worst, then carry on. You may be very happy to be judged by your work. Just bear in mind that in these days of tight budgets the loudest voice may get the biggest budget!

the thinker

the investigator

I want answers. I especially want answers to the problems I want to solve, and opportunities I want to investigate. And I want the right answers, and I want them right now!

the shapes and shades of their personality

violet, squiggle, triangle, blue

With a squiggle streak that keeps giving them ideas, a triangle trait that keeps them on the straight and narrow, a blue streak that means they will organize their lives around turning these ideas into action, and with a violet side that lets them get quietly on with it instead of having to "waste time blabbing," then overall you can see this is a pretty strong concoction.

what are they like?

how do they act and what turns them on?

Investigators love to explore all the connections they can see. They are highly likely to see the "Big Picture" in whatever they do, be able to organize people, and put plans in place to get things done. With something of a disregard for people-based things that are not in the vocabulary of a triangle (unless of course it is "logical" to do them, like recruit, motivate, etc) then they can get on with the tough, hard tasks of defining, refining, and mining the worth out of new and exciting possibilities.

chef's notes

With a single-minded purpose of spirit and something of a go-it-alone approach (unless logic dictates they need a team), they will set themselves goals (the triangle and blue part), and expect that they and those around them will meet those goals. With their ability to organize themselves and others they are pretty likely to succeed.

the helper
I want to give.
I'll do all I can to help others achieve their goals too.

the shapes and shades of their personality

yellow, squiggle, circle, blue
Their yellow makes them outgoing. Their squiggle means they can see the "Big Picture" and the options that will help them get there. Their circle makes them people people; their blue means that their actions will be decisive.

what are they like?

how do they act and what turns them on?
The helper as a leader of a charity springs to mind, not that "helper" types need to be typecast in the job they do. Yet the job they do will be based around people. They will base their life and work around the needs of others and their own need to make a difference and do something decisive.

Blue circles are natural leaders; with the yellow need for outside stimulation, they will be able to stand up and say their piece. Usually, because they are friendly people, they will take others with them on their journey through life. Being good leaders and thoughtful of others they are likely to help others get what they want by training, coaching, and counselling them (all good HR stuff). And let's not forget, this is helping them get what they want too!

the helper

the butterfly
I love ideas and people and will flit between both.

the shapes and shades of their personality

yellow, squiggle, circle, red

Their yellow makes them outgoing. Their squiggle means they can see a world of possibilities that will let them travel anywhere. Their circle makes them people people, and their red makes them play with ideas and possibilities, which will often be people or values based.

what are they like?

how do they act and what turns them on?

Butterflies are fun to be with and great to watch. They have lots of ideas and are nice people who worry about what you think (because they hold deep values and are concerned for others). Their squiggle side, combined with that playful red, will have them flitting from idea to idea.

Do you have a problem? Their circle nature will ensure they come bounding up to help you solve it. Beware though, without the boxy thoroughness and the blue organizational skills, the idea may be just that, an idea. When asked later about why it didn't work, they may sulk and wonder why themselves, but they may never quite work it out. Not that they will worry for long as they flit off to something new!

> ### chef's notes
> Like loose cannon types they are full of boundless energy but more sensitive to their impact on others. This will not stop them believing deeply in whatever cause they happen to be following (at the time!).

the butterfly

the watcher

I like harmony on the inside and out. If I can help give others the ideas and ways to make their lives better I will, but I won't force myself on them.

the shapes and shades of their personality

violet, squiggle, circle, red

Life is full of possibilities, full of different ways of living it, full of different people who pursue their way in life in completely different ways. What a joy for a violet squiggle to watch people go by, observing the patterns of their behaviors and how they interact with each other. With an inner strength driven by values rather than logic (coming from their circle trait) they will be ever interested in people. Their red trait will ensure they will play with all the ideas and concepts about people, and forever be fascinated in what others do. At their core they will want to use all their ideas to ensure that what happens to them is exactly what they feel is right.

what are they like?

how do they act and what turns them on?

What is important to you may not be important to the watcher but they will be fascinated by whatever you do. You may not be aware that they are studying you in particular, or people in general, for they are of course violet. Or you may be aware of their fascination for all things "people," as they may have chosen a profession that allows them to watch people. And maybe even to help and advise them about achieving either that mystical thing our watchers might call inner peace, or more simply be better trained to meet with the needs of living.

chef's notes

With their red trait allowing them not to be judgmental, and their ability to wait until the last minute to have all the possibilities examined, they won't pre-judge the outcome. They are just watching, quietly, as they are violet. What they may do, if they let you "up close and personal," is share their ideas with you and allow you to decide what to do with your life. But watch out – if your way of dealing with things conflicts for any reason with theirs then be ready for an interesting debate!

the watcher

the guardian angel

I get on with what I must do, no fuss, no noise. I like to lead from behind rather than from the front, helping people to deliver what's in our communities best interest.

the shapes and shades of their personality

violet, squiggle, circle, blue

With an inner strength driven by ideas and possibilities (their squiggle trait), and with an outer drive to organize their life and the lives of others around their deep values, the guardian angel can be the quiet leader others love to follow. For they display all those characteristics of the strong, silent type but with a soft people focus. Their violet and blue side means they will quietly organize people to get things done while showing the way with their ability to see the future.

what are they like?

how do they act and what turns them on?

Give me someone with a vision and I will show you someone who has followers. For most people who believe they cannot see into the future will be happy to follow someone who can. The guardian angels have an ability to show a world of possibilities based on sound people values and this, together with their blue organizational skills, provides the basis for a quiet form of leadership.

> **chef's notes**
>
> Whether you are a circle or a triangle, if you feel or think that doing the right thing is important then you will look up to someone with the traits that demonstrate a commitment to others and an ability to get on with making good things happen. These are the traits of the guardian angel. Not that we are saying the rest of us are not ethical, and not that their version of good things may be very different from yours. We're not talking walking on water types, just about violet, squiggles with circle, and blue there too!

guardian angel

the friend in need

I want to help. I want to be involved in what is going on. And I'll (usually) do it with a smile as my plans and actions are people based.

the shapes and shades of their personality

yellow, box, circle, blue

Their yellow makes them outgoing. Their box means they are in the here and now, and they are happy to do what is takes, however detailed or hands on. Their circle makes them people people and their blue means that their actions, usually decisive, will be people or values based.

what are they like?

how do they act and what turns them on?

Everyone wants a friend when they are in need. Here is one who will listen to all your problems, concerns, ambitions, and be delighted to let you take all the time in the world to do it, for they will love to hear all the detail, especially when it concerns you and anyone else around you. In fact (a good boxy word), they are pretty likely to put themselves in a position where they are able to listen to other people, be it in teams, in clubs, or on the local board of something or other.

> ## chef's notes
>
> Your friend in need is likely to have a smile on their face, and if you watch you will see them tilt their head to one side to listen to you better (a body language trait of many circles). Together with other circle traits, like encouraging nods, leaning towards you with an intent look on their face as they hang on your every word, lots of "uhhh hmmm's" and "really, did they do that?", you will find their spontaneous friendliness infectious. Doesn't it just make you want to be so, sooo… nice, like them?

the friend

in need

the coach

I'll give you good advice. I'll show you what to do and how to do it. I enjoy doing things for people. Just don't expect too much "future stuff," or big picture, or conceptual thinking, or a host of ideas.

the shapes and shades of their personality

yellow, box, circle, red

Their yellow makes them outgoing. Their box means they are in the here and now, and they are happy to do what is takes, however detailed or hands on. Their circle makes them people people and their red means that they will have fun with their actions.

what are they like?

how do they act and what turns them on?

Don't you just love those easy-going types who get along, especially if they are one of those life and soul of the party types. Well, our yellow, box, circle, and red friends can be like that. They are people who like doing things, especially when it means doing them with others – team games come to mind. The red part of them means they like to play at what they do, not that they can't be serious at playing, you only need to think how competitive sport is. That's because to a box the detail like "how many hundredths of a second can I shave off the time?" is really important.

They will be good coaches as they will enjoy watching the progress of others and delight in being able to help. They will know who needs to do what, what needs to go where, where everyone needs to be when, when everyone needs to do what. Ask them for the theoretical reasons why things need to be done and you may find you get more answers back on the what, how, when, and where!

the coach

the supporter

I don't brag about what I do. I just love to watch others and help them do what I can to make them successful.

the shapes and shades of their personality

violet, box, circle, red

Their violet trait and circle inner strength gives them a deep sense of values. They have a need to be liked by others as well as liking to watch others in action – they love nothing more than being in the "here and now" with people. This all makes them great people watchers. Their box side means they will do things that need to be done – but with their red trait it will be "sometime," usually last minute!

what are they like?

how do they act and what turns them on?

You can think of the supporter like the fan of the game, the music, the writer, etc. They aren't on the stage, someone else is. They won't be "up there" stirring things up, being controversial, being seen. They will be in the background. With a sense of values and inward focus that makes them the "quiet one." They will be "there for you" when you need it and "rooting for you" whether you want it or not, whether you recognize they are around or not – for they are on your side.

And the danger here for the majority of people who are yellow, is that they won't think to involve the supporters and all other violets. For yellows "saying my piece" comes naturally. And if you don't say your piece – well that's your problem! So two things need to happen. Number 1 – yellows need to stop, and ask questions of violets, even give them more time to process their thinking. Number 2 – violets need to assert themselves more, because yellows aren't that likely to do Number 1!

the supporter

the rock
You can count on me.

the shapes and shades of their personality

violet, box, circle, blue

Their violet makes them inward focussed and their circle gives them a sense of values based around people that can go deep. Together with their box side and blue organizational ability, they will be the cornerstone for any team.

what are they like?

how do they act and what turns them on?

Once again, like the pragmatist, with the box trait as their inner strength, and with their reserved violet nature, the rock is the person you need to get things done, quietly and efficiently. They will do it well with no fuss and no demands on other people's time for (as they see it) unnecessary social interaction.

What their circle side does gives them is a deeply committed sense of doing their bit, of playing their part, and delivering their best. This is the external driver that you will see. Their concern for others and their need for any team they are in to work as a team, is more evident than their inner strength, which is their focus on detail. Yet when it comes to delivering the detail, they will deliver, time and time again, with the same degree of attention and concentration that will ensure you get what you asked for. Why? Because they will worry about what others think about them, and they won't feel good if others around them don't feel good about them or their work.

the sorter
Whatever needs sorting I will sort it.
I'll get the job done. Simple as that.

the shapes and shades of their personality

yellow, box, triangle, blue
With this combination of detail and decision making they may do some of it themselves, their boxy bit, and they may get others to do it, their triangle and blue bit. They will be "out there," their yellow bit, but it will get done!

what are they like?

how do they act and what turns them on?
With a penchant for decision making based on facts "they know to be true" our sorters will make sure that things are, well, sorted. "Let's get down to business; let's sort the wheat from the chaff; let's make sure we are on track and everything is in place for doing what needs to be done." I can just hear them saying these boxy and triangley words.

With a yellow bent for being where the action is, they will be organizing others as only a good admin manager or purchasing controller might – not that I am labeling them, oh no, just giving an example of people's perception of what an admin manager or purchasing controller might be like!

They won't be slow to act either. Blue triangles with any of the other traits will decide quickly, because that's what turns them on, making decisions. The chances are they will make good decisions because their judgment will be based on the "facts," unlike the squiggles who will base decisions on theory and an idea things might work.

---

chef's notes
If you are stuck on a desert island with a sorter then rest assured you are in good hands; they will help build the shelter, and soon have an inventory of food and a roster for work to be done.

the sorter

the fixer
Leave it to me, I'll put it right for you.

the shapes and shades of their personality

yellow, box, triangle, red

Their yellow makes them outgoing so they will be working or playing hard with others. Their red makes them play with the things you can touch, see, and fix. Their triangle means they will be driven by the logical need to put right what they see as wrong and do well at what they do well, like practical jobs, sport, and games – things that to them are real, here and now.

what are they like?

how do they act and what turns them on?

Our fixers are great to have around when you need someone who has their wits about them to make things go right. If they do need to think about things, they will go away and think things through on their own, and then they will come out and move into action mode. Their red trait allows them to deal with whatever comes along last minute. In fact, rather than being organized, they would much rather deal with those down-to-earth, boxy-type activities as and when they appear.

With a triangle rather than circle focus, logic, and thinking will steer them to practical jobs which may or may not involve people. Not much will phase them as they are flexible enough to deal with whatever life throws at them.

> ### chef's notes
> And so we come to the end of our yellows. We move on to the violets where all the endings like squiggle, triangle, red are a mirror image of the yellow traits but Boy! are they really, really, really different.

the fixer

the bystander
Leave me alone, then I'll put it right for you.

the shapes and shades of their personality

violet, box, triangle, red

Their violet makes them inward focussed so they will be content with their own company, or the company of a few, very select and trusted friends or colleagues. Like their fixer counterpart, their red makes them play with analyzing the things you can touch, see, and fix. BUT, and it is a big but, they are really clever. Because (like you will see with all violets) they don't want you to see or know what they are really like. So they hide their core trait, you could call it their real inner strength. It is their triangle that really drives them. That means they will be fired by the logical need to solve problems. So rather than being fixers they will be the bystander who tells people what needs fixing!

what are they like?

how do they act and what turns them on?

Compare our bystanders to our fixers. Only one change of shade and what a difference. Whilst our fixers are great to have around when things go wrong, and want to be around in sport, the chances are you won't see our bystander around much at all. With their clever triangle core (that they hide) and their ability to see the facts, the figures, the problems, and then come up with the solutions, they will be working away (on their own) to give you the answers to the questions that you have. You can also expect to get those out of the blue one-liners that sum up a situation and that you wish you could have said yourself.

chef's notes
Bystanders won't be the life and soul of the party but their ability to deliver advice that works commands the respect of others.

the bystander

the pragmatist
**I'll leave you alone and do a good job of what I do.
I'll also do whatever I think is necessary.**

the shapes and shades of their personality

violet, box, triangle, blue
Like the bystander, and all other violets, their violet makes them inward focussed so they will be content with their own company, or the company of a few, very select and trusted friends or colleagues. With their visible strength of triangle and their inner strength of box they will be seen to be great at thinking through all the detail. Their blue gives them the ability to be organized and well able to deal with the job in hand in a logical, step-by-step way that starts at point 1 on the list and finishes (in sequence) at point 10, quietly. Compare that to a yellow squiggle who may start at point 10, go back and try to do points 3 and 4, and then go off to do something else entirely, making lots of noise while doing it!

what are they like?

how do they act and what turns them on?
When you need to get things done with no fuss, no noise, no leaping around, and no need for close supervision (once they know what they are doing) then the pragmatist is your person. They will start and finish the job, and be happy to be totally accountable for making sure it's done, in a way that they will be satisfied with. They may over-engineer it, they may deliver more than you asked for, or even wanted, but they will deliver what they think is right, needed, and to a standard they (not you) are happy with. Oh, and if the world is collapsing around you, or them while they are working away, don't be surprised if they don't notice. Their focus on logic and their inner strength around attention to detail means that they will be focussed – really focussed.

the pragmatist

the unknown

I just have no idea what I am. Sometimes I'm this. Sometimes I'm that. On my "tests" I am borderline on this, not sure they are right on that, confused about the other.

the shapes and shades of their personality

In some of the psychology tests some people are not sure if the descriptions they are given apply to them. In "shapes and shades" I have never found anyone who doesn't relate to them. I have found the odd person who doesn't want to enter into the spirit of them and who questions their validity. Apart from having run sessions on them with thousands of people I have no statistical evidence of their validity.

So if you don't want to or can't place yourself in any of the boxes, or squiggles, then you will just have to forgo a language that lets people relate to who you are, how to communicate effectively with you, and how to debate and discuss how you can work together in your different ways.

You must forever remain – the unknown. (But beware it won't stop others guessing what your personality is like, with or without "shapes and shades"; you can still be described by a whole host of names whether you like it or not!)

what are they like, how do they act, and what turns them on?

What do you do if you are an unknown even after "shapes and shades" and any other test? Whilst the great thing about "shapes and shades" is that it is pretty hard not to know if you are one of the four pairs, you may find you still aren't sure if they apply as individual descriptions, or grouped in the 16 types. That's OK. There are some people I find difficult to read. So stick them in here for now. This makes for just as interesting a type as all the others! It also makes the "shapes and shades" traits really accurate, as any problem areas simply get shunted out. How's that for something devised by a squiggle. Do I hear the boxes groan, the triangles ask for proof, the violets do not want to expose their thinking (yet), the blues asking what use this all is in real life, and the circles not caring because it makes for good people watching anyway? Or am I typecasting and putting people into boxes when life is full of rich and unimaginable differences so that all this is unhelpful and downright too simple.

> ### chef's notes
> Whatever your thoughts about any of our characters, they make for great debate. I know that the many thousands of people who have been exposed to "shapes and shades" have at least found it fun!

the unknown

the shape sorter
an ice breaker

The following "how to" (steps 1 to 4) is a wonderful ice breaker for large gatherings when you want to introduce people to the idea of "shapes and shades" and get lots and lots of debate, discussion, and maybe even disagreement! The final shape sorter grid map (after step 5) is really useful for filling out a team's "shapes and shades" at the end of this exercise to create even more debate. The final result will give you a visual map of who is what and how many of each type of personality you have.

steps 1–5

You have a room full of people. You want to have some fun, create some debate, get people talking. Follow the simple procedure. Always explain: "This is just for fun. It is a communication exercise just to see how we relate to each other in our various communication styles. If at any time you want to drop out or pretend to be someone else to hide the real you, then feel free."

step 1
yellow or violet – are you driven from inside or outside?

Show the step 1 diagram. Say "If you are a 'yellow' person go to the left-hand side of the room. If you are a 'violet' person go to the right-hand side of the room." (Use the instructions on the personality profiler to help you explain how to choose the "shape and shade." When they have chosen, double check that they have chosen the right shade by showing the descriptions. Ask them to move to the correct side if they chose "wrongly." (The alternative to this method is less risky and less fun. You simple put the descriptions up, then move them to the side of the room that fits them best. Choose one alternative from now on.)

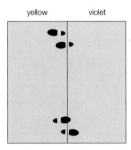

step 1 – yellow or violet
are you driven from inside or outside?

step 2
squiggle or box – are you driven by ideas or information?

While staying on the left or right for yellow or violet now get them to choose if they are squiggle or box. Squiggles go to the front of the room; boxes go to the rear. Repeat the double-check procedure with the "shape and shade" definitions – do this in steps 3 and 4 also. Try to avoid too much debate at this stage!

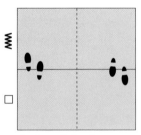

step 2 – squiggle or box
are you driven by ideas or information?

step 3
triangle or circle – are you driven by logic or values?

Get them to choose triangle or circle. Now say: "Triangles to the front if you are a squiggle and rear of the room if you are a box. Circles stay where you are." Show the diagram. There will probably be a great deal of confusion here. Live with it: this was designed by a squiggle (me, and I can make it work, most of the time!). Repeat the double-check procedure. If they want to change shape or shade let them! This creates more confusion and fun (unless you may be overly boxy!).

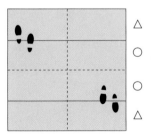

step 3 – triangle or circle
are you driven by logic or values?

step 4
blue or red – are you driven by plans or do you like to play?

Get them to choose blue or red. Now you say: "Blue people to the far left if you are yellow and go to the far right of the room if you are violet." A final double check here showing the blue and red descriptions.

You now have a room full of people in approximately 16 zones. You now need to show them what all this means. Go to step 5.

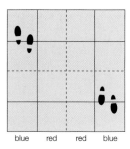

blue   red   red   blue

step 4 – blue or red
are you driven by plans
or do you like to play?

step 5
now they are sorted

You can do a number of things:

- Get them to use their name badges (or sticky computer labels) to write their four personal "shapes and shades," eg yellow, squiggle, triangle, red. Watch and see how much personal discussion this creates! "I didn't know you were like that!" "Wow, as squiggles we are so similar but we are also very different with our blue and red traits."

- Depending on the number of people (and it works best if they are a team) get them to come to the front and fill in their type on the shape sorter grid map (it's on the next two pages). You can use this to record and highlight the range and number of characters.

- You can show the descriptions of the 16 characters given in the character complementer. This will give people a summary of what their overall result looks like.

- You can then use these descriptions as a final triple check to see if their character matches the full descriptions. Move them to the "correct" box where necessary.

- You can get people from the same or different characters to talk not just about their similarities and differences but how they can operate as a team and overcome any difficulties.

- The main point of the exercise is to use the results to create lots of debate. "We are mostly squiggles – who will get any work done!" "We have no coaches – what does this mean for us?" "With so many blue people is this why we are all trying to manage each other and clashing?"

My "to do " list • the shape sorter

shape sorter grid map

	yellow		violet	
	the boss	the loose cannon	the thinker	the investigator
	the helper	the butterfly	the watcher	the guardian angel
	the friend in need	the coach	the supporter	the rock
	the sorter	the fixer	the bystander	the pragmatist
	blue	red	red	blue

my "to do" list

fill in my team names

	yellow		violet		
〰	Y≷△B	Y≷△R	V≷△R	V≷△B	△
	Y≷○B	Y≷○R	V≷○R	V≷○B	○
□	Y□○B	Y□○R	V□○R	V□○B	○
	Y□△B	Y□△R	V□△R	V□△B	△
	blue	red	red	blue	

My "to do" list • the shape sorter

what are you thinking?
and how are you feeling?

- **three critical success checks on the climate**
  When you need to know what they are saying, doing, look like.

- **three critical success checks on the culture**
  When you need to know what people are thinking, feeling, believing.

- **the "Yes!" factor**
  What we all want overall.

- **now for a fortune cookie**
  The hundred best companies to work for.

critical to success

how to check climate and culture

Employee attitude surveys, telephone research, focus groups, exit interviews, face-to-face discussions, 360° appraisals. all intended to do one thing – find out stuff. But is it the right stuff and if you find it out, can you do anything with it? Too often the answer is negative. The leaders and managers in the organization simply want to know if everything they are doing to inform and inspire is turning into actions that generate returns.

This book has been full of simple recipes – now it's time to see if they are working. The measures of success can be tested with two "instant" temperature gauges to see if, first, your climate has changed as you follow the new recipes for success and, second, if the changes in your climate are creating a change in culture.

1 climate checks

There are three critical success factors you need to assess under the "visible" issues that make up the climate of organizations. These are what people:

- do
- say
- look like.

And if these are working the great thing for you is that your culture will follow. How do you know? Do a culture check next.

2 culture checks

There are three critical success factors you need to assess under the "hidden" issues that make up the culture of the organization. We have talked of these under the headings of what people:

- think
- feel
- believe.

the "yes!" factor

The final and simplest check of all on whether or not you have the results you want.

now for a fortune cookie

A quick quote from *Fortune* magazine on "The Hundred Best Companies to Work For."

what's up?

my "to do" list:
climate checks

it's time to find out if all these recipes and ingredients are working well, over-cooked, or are not working at all!

what to SAY and DO

Ask these three simple, easy questions for three reasons:

- to get a steer on how much people are acting on something
- to give you the basis for deeper discussion on why they have given this score
- to give you the basis for discussing what could be done differently – by you or them.

Ask these too at any time, either in writing or verbally. Ask them at the end of an e-mail, in conversation, in a formal survey, in the corridor, in the bar after work, in the restaurant, at the bus stop – just ask them!

You can use these questions around any issue/topic/subject/problem/opportunity, etc and check whether people think you are "walking the talk" or others are doing and saying the right things.

---

climate check – what you can see, hear, touch

I/he/she/we/they SAY
I/he, etc SAYS good/not good things about... Score 1 2 3 4 5
WHY do you think I/he, etc says good/not good things about...?

For example: He says good/not good things about **my work**. Score **2**
WHY? **Because I don't think he likes me and it shows!**

I/he/she/we/they DO
"I/he, etc DOES DO things/DOES NOT DO things about..." Score 1 2 3 4 5
WHY do you think I/he, etc does not do things about...?

For example: We do/don't do things about **living our brand**. Score **4**
WHY? **Because we are true to our values, like caring for our customers.**

I/he/she/we/they LOOK
"I/he, etc LOOKS good/ DOESN'T LOOK good about..." Score 1 2 3 4 5
WHY do you think I/he, etc looks good/ doesn't look good about...?

For example: **Our offices** do/don't look good. Score **3**
WHY? **Our reception areas are great, but the cubicles are like Dilbert cartoons!**

---

chef's notes

If you think they are simple – go try them. By starting to ask questions like these, you are starting to do and say things differently and instantly signaling a climate change. You might just be surprised at what comes out of it. And if you are afraid of the answers, be even more afraid of not knowing what they are!

And if your climate is changing then your culture will follow. How do you know? Move on now to the three critical checks on culture.

are you

boiling over?

my "to do" list:
culture checks

now you'll find out if all this "walk the talk" is working!

what to do

Ask these three simple, easy questions for three reasons:

- to get a steer on how much people think/feel/believe about something
- to give you the basis for deeper discussion on why they have given this score
- to give you the basis for discussing what could be done differently – by you or them.

Ask them at any time, either in writing or verbally. Ask them at the end of an e-mail, in conversation, in a formal survey, in the corridor, in the bar after work, in the restaurant, at the bus stop – just ask them!

You can use these questions around any issue/topic/subject/problem/opportunity, etc.

---

culture check (the stuff you can't see)

I THINK
"Do you THINK… is/is not great." Score 1 2 3 4 5

WHY do you think… is/is not great?

For example: Do you think our vision is/is not great? Score 2.

WHY? I think it is lousy! It's more like a corporate wish list. Especially as the competition is knocking us for six.

I FEEL
"Do you feel good/not good about…" Score 1 2 3 4 5

WHY do you feel good/not good about…?

For example: Do you feel good/not good about working here? Score 4.

WHY? I just love it. What a place. Everyone is wonderful.

I BELIEVE
"Do you believe/don't believe…" Score 1 2 3 4 5

WHY do you believe/not believe…?

For example: Do you believe/don't believe we will survive this recession. Score 3.

WHY? Deep down I have to say I am really really not convinced we will make it.

There you have it – your fastest reference guide ever on climate and culture. Would you like an even faster way of checking success? Of course! Try the "yes!" factor coming next. It's the last recipe and the most powerful indicator that things are working. Good luck with it all, bonne chance, and bon appetit.

too hot to handle

the "yes!" factor

what's your score out of ten:	_____ /10
what's your company score:	_____ /10
what's your CEO's score:	_____ /10

ingredients

Imagine you only have one way of testing motivation, morale, employee satisfaction, passion, trust, commitment, etc. How do you do that? The answer lies in the obvious, something you can see, something you can hear, something you can watch happening (or not), every minute of the day in your organization. "What is it?" and "I want it," I hear you say.

For the past 20 years businesses have been measuring employee satisfaction, often only on a yearly basis, certainly not monthly, definitely not daily, and without a shadow of a doubt not on a minute-by-minute basis. These employee satisfaction surveys have tended to reveal one thing: that in organizations across the globe the satisfaction is usually about five out of ten. It's been five out of ten for the last 20 years. Despite the incredible advances in our ability to reach people with communications systems ranging from e-mails to web-casting, employee satisfaction hasn't improved – it has worsened. We ask employees what they think about the organization, its vision, its goals, its practices, its products, its services. We ask them what they feel about the organization's values, its leadership, its management, its culture. But are we asking the right things in the right way? Yes, if what you want to do is check hearts and minds, ie culture. Absolutely no, if you want to check the climate within organizations.

So how do you check climate? Try the method below. See if it isn't intuitively right for you. If you want a technical term for it you can call it reading body language; you can call it listening out for organizational linguistics; you can describe it as emotional responses to psychological and intellectual challenges, opportunities, or threats. I call it the "yes!" factor. It contains some, many, or all of the ten dynamic emotions in business and it manifests itself in what people say, what they do, and what they look like when they're doing it.

method

Imagine the most exciting moment in your life, from winning millions to being given the job of your dreams or discovering the cure to every illness ever. Try leaping in the air, punching your fist as high as you can, with a huge smile on your face, and shouting as loud as you can "YES!" That is a ten out of ten "yes!" factor.

Do you want everyone to have a ten out of ten "yes!" factor? "YES!" you say? Over to you! Off you go! You first! The rest will follow. I put it to you that every great idea, every great leader, every challenge overcome, occurred with liberal doses of this factor. Visions, missions, values – great stuff; the "yes!" factor is what makes them all work!

chef's notes
The results will speak, dance, and sing for themselves!

now for a fortune cookie

time to sit down with a great cup of coffee – here is where you get a fortune cookie to tell your future!

Maybe you are asking if you really need to do (or want to do) all this climate and culture stuff? Well, here's a final fortune cookie that shows you that all the great companies are using our cookbook recipes to deliver great results.

The following are two short extracts from "The Hundred Best Companies To Work For" (*Fortune* magazine, January 2001). Maybe reading these extracts will help predict if you too will be with an organization that thinks getting the right climate, culture, and mix of people is important. Will this fortune cookie tell you if you will be with an organization where they SAY things differently, DO things differently, and LOOK different? If you are with one of the Top 100 you will be!

the hundred best companies to work for

how the work place was won

You may think of the story of the work place as early Workingman creeping, caveman-like, out of the dingy factory and into the lighted cubicle, but it's a bit more complicated than that. Even in the old days, back when profit sharing was deemed a radical concept and paid vacations were considered an unattainable luxury, there were great places to work. No, they didn't offer massages to pieceworkers, or sabbaticals to stevedores, but these companies did make the fascinating discovery that improving working conditions and treating employees like human beings actually paid dividends, and kept a union of rabble-rousers at bay into the bargain. At four companies, Procter and Gamble, IBM, Hewlett-Packard, and Wal-Mart, enlightened leadership has created work places that stood out during various epochs of the 20th century.

how we pick the 100 best

To gain a spot among this year's 100 best, the 234 candidates were willing to undergo considerable scrutiny. First, they agreed to allow us to survey a randomly selected group of their employees (at least 250 employees per firm).

This year, a record 36,106 employees filled out the Great Place To Work Trust Index here is that really important "secret ingredient" again, trust) … an employee survey that evaluates trust in management, pride (another emotion) in work and the company, and camaraderie. Some 14,338 of this year's respondents also provided the individual written comments about their work places, and more than 500 other centers e-mailed or phoned us with their views.

The survey and comments account for two-thirds of our scoring. The remainder of the score is determined by each company's responses to the institute's culture (chef's notes - the result of climate) audit, in which it explains its philosophy (chef's notes – what they THINK, FEEL, BELIEVE) and practices (chef's notes – what they SAY, DO, and how they LOOK) and include supplementary materials, employee handbooks, company newsletters, and videos.

ask yourself – how good is my company to work for?

the future...
over to you

addendum: everything has changed

food to feed the spirit

Since September 11 2001 a lot has happened – not least of which "everything has changed." This addendum is here to serve as a guide to just some of the ways that leaders, managers, and people in business will need to SAY, DO, and LOOK differently at "the way we do things around here." Why? Because we are now THINKING, FEELING, and most importantly BELIEVING differently. We are thinking about safety, security, and the consequences of everything we are doing within our businesses and with our brands (eg spreading our brand across the globe). We are feeling insecure about travel, parcels in the post, our future with our jobs. We are believing that staying at home is infinitely better than staying late at the office.

So what do we SAY, DO, and LOOK like as we handle the aftermath. Much of what we have seen in this cookbook is no longer, I believe, a "nice to have," its relevance is magnified. Why? Because who wants to be operating in an environment that leaves a lot to be desired when the stakes for working at all have been raised so high?

And, on top of what we have covered already, there is more to do in the current environment when crisis and conflict are now par for the course. This section, "Food to Feed The Spirit," is intended to help people through the tough job of communicating in a tough environment.

food to feed the spirit recipes

- Planning for long-term change
- Clarity of the message in a crisis
- Reinforcing the message in a crisis
- Emphasis on facts – the 6Cs framework for structuring high-concern communication
- Emphasis on feeling – a model for talking, listening, asking questions, eliciting responses
- Poison mushroom – negative versus positive communication (1N = 3P)

workingthrough.org

The material below is from the pro bono website workingthrough.org set up by our business, our colleagues in the WPP organization (like Hill and Knowlton, Ogilvy), and colleagues and academics from all over the world. This site was set up to help and guide businesses and communication professionals through the concerns and issues of the traumatic events of September 11 2001, and the economic, social, political, and personal fallout. The message it gives is that we now have to say, do, and look at things in a completely new way, not just reacting to the crisis and any future attacks, but also how we "change" to meet the challenges ahead. We all will be thinking, feeling, and believing differently. What will we say, do, and look like as we go about changing? This section is intended to help. The recipes are adapted from the help and advice provided on **workingthrough.org**

workingthrough.org
home page September 24:09:2001
Introduction by Kevin Thomson, FCIM, ABC, Honorary Professor Birmingham University Business School, President MCA – WPP Group, and Professor Jon White, Adviser on Communication and Public Relations to Henley Management College and Stirling University.

This isn't just about crisis communication at any given point in time. We must now consider the notion that for many aspects of people's life, not least employment, "nothing will be the same."

Crisis communication has in the past helped businesses respond to a specific issue at a point in time – from poisoned products to fires and explosions, from oil spills to maritime disasters. Events have been specific to a business or industry and have tended to have individual effects on the operations of a company and its people and community.

What the events of September 11 2001 have done is to redefine the meaning of a crisis and therefore of crisis communication. Previously, "crisis" in business meant "unexpected bad publicity" – and the consequent threat to reputation. Now it means a threat to your own personal safety and that of your colleagues, and potentially your family. It also implies a threat to the principles on which democracy is built and the foundations of business itself.

Continued...

leading the way

planning for long-term change

When businesses plan for long-term change, such as re-structuring, mergers and acquisitions, and global expansion, they frequently use the well-documented "change curve" to plan activities. Long-term changes like this involve major shifts in the way people in businesses think, believe, and act, and it often involves redefining a company's visions, missions, and values. Right now, both the ability to achieve long-term change and deliver a company's vision, mission, and values are under attack, because the attack on America was an attack on "Western" business and culture. Businesses will need to plan their communication in a way that will support the longer-term changes which will inevitably arise and affect both their businesses and their people for a long time after this immediate crisis has ended.

crisis AND change communication – we move from a change curve to a new "crisis curve," driven by both crisis and change

In the past, specific crises were rarely the instigators of long-term change in business. Now we have a situation where we need not just one form of communication – either change or crisis – but both. And we face issues so broad and all-encompassing that no previous model or process for business communication within organizations has existed.

a new language will emerge

As we enter a new era, it's up to every individual to look at what they say, do, and how they and their businesses communicate. This is a time where business and politics, economics and religion, trade and countries, brands and their brand ambassadors, are all mixing into one big system. Each element is no longer operating separately but is seen to be related to the others and all must start to operate together. A new language will emerge. What follows are some recipes to all help people through the immediate crisis.

going the distance

clarity of the message in a crisis

We introduced the WHY mnemonic in this cookbook as a tool to structure both spoken and written communication. Here's a reminder for introducing your communication in a crisis.

ingredients

When you have to write, say, or deliver a short sharp message what do you do? Launch into it without a thought? Try this. Write out the WHY mnemonic first – formulate your messages against the three headings – What, Hooks, Your Aim. Then you can deliver your message knowing you have thought through what you want to say, what they want to hear, and what you want them to do. You can therefore concentrate more on their response than on your thinking or delivery.

What – what you want to get across

- **One main message**
  For example… "I have to inform you that unfortunately/sadly/tragically/ we have news that…"

- **Three sub-headings maximum**
  There are three key points that I want to let you know, they are 1….2….3….

- **Finally, remember the mind can't compute "don't."**
  Don't say "Don't panic" – everyone panics! Do say "Keep calm."

Hooks – what's in it for them

- **Give them the personal benefits they will receive.**

- **Address the personal issues.**
  If you use the word "you" then you will be talking about their issues, eg "You will be concerned about…"

- **Address emotional as well as intellectual concerns.**
  "You must be feeling…"

- **Use words/phrases they use and keep the language simple.**
  Avoid jargon like "We have a situation/scenario here." Instead say "What is happening is…"

Your aim – what you want them to do

Tell them the actions you want them to undertake to achieve your goals. (Yes, tell them – you have done all the "involving" part, now you want results.) They also want your leadership.

any questions?

What do you do if there are any questions?

- KISS (Keep It Short and Simple) their questions.
  Structure your answers with a short empathetic opening, eg "Thank you for raising that, I can understand your worries…"

- If you can, give two supporting facts to any statements you may make. Any more overloads the circuits or leads people to think "she doth protest too much."

---

chef's notes

Remember – in high-concern situations, people can only retain three pieces of information. This is why the WHY technique is so powerful – and the whole point of WHY is to end up with ACTIONS that people can get going on.

getting across

reinforcing the message in a crisis

In a high-concern situation – especially one that has been on TV and repeated time and time again (think of the number of times people saw the World Trade Center being attacked) strong visual images are often burned into people's minds. In the same way, using visualization reinforces messages and aids retention. It helps counteract the negative pictures we too often see on TV. Remember in real life – without TV – you would normally only see an event occur once. Visualization of new and positive images helps to build new pictures and break through existing images as well as the mental noise of words, words, words, and worry, worry, worry.

ingredients

Use images you create as often as you can to demonstrate a point. Get them to create images themselves. Use words like "imagine…," "see…," "picture this…" Use all the senses and the visual, auditory, and kinesthetic words that are associated with them like feel, hear, touch (all the things that NLP teaches).

- "What do you see yourself doing in six months' time?"
- "What do you feel about the current situation?"
- Use images that can evoke strong associations, eg car (need to a jump start; fine-tuning); garden (sowing seeds; planting ideas).
- Build in anecdotes and storytelling. They are very powerful (and can be true or fictional).
- Where you can, use photographs, video (video streaming via intranets is a great example), and where you can use pictures, graphics, charts, and graphs to translate figures and messages.
- Avoid formulaic presentations – stories are better.
- Remember a picture is worth a thousand words.

Here's an example of something you might be saying in a crisis planning session: "Imagine yourself in another crisis – what do you see yourself doing? Do you picture yourself doing what some of those brave firemen, rescue workers, and "ordinary" employees did? Can you feel what they felt? Now, how will you, your colleagues, and your business react in a similar situation?"

Being able to picture the outcomes of situations will help prepare you for the reality. In many ways, it is TV and the movies which provide us with the "stories" that help us cope with real life. In this situation, real life is infinitely worse than the Hollywood disaster movies. Visualization will help people cope with the reality of what has happened and what may yet come. Visualization in our own businesses is as much a part of communication as words.

concern

emphasis on facts –
the 6C's framework for structuring high-concern communication

The **WHY** mnemonic allows you to do a "quick" introduction for any communication. When you need to cover a topic in depth that requires the facts then try the 6C's. Your messages will be more effective by applying the following structure in the spoken and written word. Every element of this structure is based on classic communication skills – and a good dose of intuitive reasoning.

ingredients – the 6C's

1 **Care** – start with a brief empathetic statement to set the tone.
  - "I understand why you feel this way."
  - "I can imagine how you are feeling."

2 **Cut to the chase** – come to the point with a clear statement outlining the decision.
  - "Getting to the point about what we need to be thinking/doing/planning/deciding..."
  - "We all know we need to..."

3 **Criteria** – give two reasons or facts for this decision (no more no less).
  - "Let me explain the rationale for this..."
  - "Let me explain why..."

4 **Choices** – address concerns (researched or assumed) and outline options.
  Use a maximum of three messages.
  - "What this means for you…"
  - "In the future..."

5 **Check understanding** – repeat your main message.
  Even better get them to repeat it for you.
  - "What have we said so far..."
  - "Most importantly, what do you think we need to do?"

6 **Commitment** – outline what happens next and refer to other names/sources to back up your commitment to help.
  - "What will happen now is..."
  - "I am going to make sure that..."

the 6 C's – an example

Your company has responded to a crisis situation and people are saying that they are left out of the loop and want the information more quickly.

Care "I understand why you feel that way and we are doing something about it, including talking with you all now."

Criteria "Let me explain why we did it: first we wanted to wait until we could give you the whole truth and second we wanted to make sure that people affected heard it first."

Concerns "In the future we'll be able to communicate more fully and more quickly, and as a first step we'll be handing out a bulletin which summarizes everything I've said today."

continued on next page...

knowing what to do

Check "As I just said, from now on I want to make sure we keep you in the picture. Is everyone clear?"

Commitment "And you've not only got my word for it. I know that John Smith and the leadership team are equally committed, as are all our managers, to exercising due professional care every step of the way throughout the current situation."

more phrases you might use

You can apply this framework in one-to-one situations or in team meetings and briefings.

Care – show you understand that your people have concerns.
- "I know you're hearing snatches of information about changes..."
- "I realize this causes you concern, and that rumors can feel threatening and are confusing things even more..."
- "I realize I may not have all the answers at this early stage, but I want to share what I can and help you/everyone reach the same level of understanding."

Cut to the chase – clearly explain what this is all about.
- "I think the best thing is to tell you straight…"
- "We have some facts you need to know..."
- "I'm very sorry to have to tell you..."
- "Let me come straight to the point…"

Criteria – help your people understand why this is happening, and why it's a good thing.
- "We've made this very difficult decision based on a number of factors but mainly it's because..."
- "Let me put this decision into a bigger context first."

Choices – suggest "what this means for you" including down-sides as well as up-sides.
- "You'll be getting a lot of detailed information over the coming days and weeks, but the main news for you is that you will have several options open to you."
- "What this means is that you'll be getting a letter outlining x, y, z."

Check understanding – recap your key messages.
- "We know this was bad news, I've covered 1…2…3… and there is also some good news for our business, good news for customers, and some good news for you."
- "Before the events we had a huge opportunity for global expansion, we are not stopping our plans, however we are..."

Commitment – let your people know what to expect next.
- "There will be more information following this meeting."
- "Please will you now speak to your line manager if you want to raise anything on a personal or *ad hoc* basis."
- "You will all have an opportunity to raise questions at the town hall and team meetings."
- "We have a massive commitment to ongoing communication – expect to hear from us, and we want to hear from you."

in times of change

emphasis on feeling –
a model for talking, listening, asking questions, eliciting responses

In a crisis, especially one where there is a tragedy involving loss of life then the golden rule is simple – let people "talk, talk, talk" and make sure you "listen, listen, listen."

let them talk – then really listen

Ask open questions to encourage people to open up. Start slowly with a question like "How are you feeling?" Everyone can tell you what they are feeling. What they are thinking may be more difficult to get them to say. Watch for the non-verbal clues – are they "pulling back," frowning, etc?

Notice their body language and analyze your own too – you may be able to tell instinctively where they are coming from on a much deeper plane than what is being said.

thank/restate

- "I appreciate what you are saying."
- "So what you're saying is…"
- "That's a very important point."
- "This is difficult for you, isn't it?"

agree/match

- "I can imagine how you feel."
- "I take this question very seriously."
- "I can understand how you get that impression."
- "I can see why you feel like this."

continued on next page...

letting things go

analyze/answer – begin to introduce the facts and move away from the emotions

Use questioning techniques – clarifying any specific questions:

- "What exactly causes you to feel this way?"
- "What in particular makes you say that?"
- "Help me to understand what it is you would like to see happen."
- "The best answer I can give you is…"
- "What I'll do as a result of this is…"
- "Let's agree that…"
- "I'd like you to… by (time/date)."

act

- "What I'll do as a result of this is…"
- "Let's agree that…"
- "I'd like you to… by (time/date)."

> **chef's notes**
>
> You will notice that the ingredients in this section, like elsewhere in this cookbook aren't meant as "scripts" – we know that scripting only works with actors and you aren't there to act. What they are, are introductory phrases that allow YOU to finish the sentence with the facts, the feelings, the emphasis, the decisions, etc that will take you forward. In any crisis there is one more ingredient we all need – luck. But it's funny that the harder you work at making things come right the luckier you tend to be.

Good luck.

moving on

poison mushroom –
negative versus positive communication
(1N = 3P)

This cookbook contains a number of examples of "poison mushroom" – ingredients to avoid at all costs. Negativity is one set of ingredients you should avoid. And yet being positive requires incredible levels of practice. Yet if changing your language helps steer people through some really tough times it is worth the effort. Why will this be tough? Because being positive is much harder than being negative. The good thing for you is that once you have the skills you will be able to deal with virtually any type of crisis.

Crisis is about "bad" things, often involving a threat of some description. The human mind when threatened automatically goes to the negative. People filter all negative information both verbal (what is said – be it by voice or written), and non-verbal (body language or the style of the message) in a high-concern situation. Fear plays a big part in what people think, feel, and believe. It can and does cloud judgment on hearts and minds.

Facts are overruled by emotions – before a person will want to know what you know, they have to believe you care. And in a high-concern situation negatives take on a multiplier effect regarding what people take out of any communication. This is where the 1N = 3P rule comes in.

One negative is equal to three positives (1N = 3P). Or put it the other way, in any crisis or high-concern situation "negatives" have three times the retention of any "positives" received. Your job therefore is to be 3X more positive. Difficult? You bet.

focus on the positive

the company culture cookbook

ingredients
"negatives" include:

- No – Not – Never – Nothing – None – Un – Dis – Im –.
- Words with negative association: can't, won't, mustn't,
- Words that serve to demean, like excuse, stupid, dumb.
- Words that add to the "worry level," like concern, problem, lie.

here is an example

"I am not a crook. I have nothing to hide," Richard Nixon, Watergate.

The negatives don't negate the allegation, they confirm it.

Better (if true!) to say: "I am a man of high integrity. I've told the truth." Even better to add two supporting facts.

Remember, all non-verbal cues will be interpreted negatively. The "looks," the "sighs," the frowns, etc all reinforce any message X3.

chef's notes

Here are five reasons to avoid negatives in communication and use positive statements and appearance:

1 You will divert people away from what IS by focussing on what IS NOT.

2 Negatives are more readily heard and picked up on, and retained three times longer.

3 Negatives tend to be absolutes (ie it encourages anyone who disagrees with you to find the exception) "Read my lips, no new taxes..!"

4 Negatives make you appear defensive.

5 Negativity breeds negativity – it's non-productive and attacking.

destructive power

my "to do" list:
food to feed the spirit

1 React empathetically and positively to any crisis and plan carefully for long-term change.

2 Communicate, communicate, communicate – tell them what you are going to tell them. It's a two-way street. And if you have nothing to say tell people you have nothing to say.

3 Clarity of message in a crisis – use WHY. Ask yourself WHY am I talking? Write out the WHY mnemonic before any form of quick communication. What Hooks Your aim.

4 Fact-based communication – be ready to act, act, act, act. When it comes to the facts remember the 6C's – care; cut to the chase; criteria; choices; check understanding; commitment.

5 Feelings-based communication – be ready to talk, talk, talk. When it comes to feelings remember the deeper the trauma, the more you need to let people talk, and the more you need to let them know you are listening.

new beginnings

all the guests are going home...

time to sit back and have a final cup of coffee and
reflect on what you have read, on what you have tried,
on what feedback you got, on the impact on your business

so let me ask you...

- "What was good?"
- "What could have been better?"
- "What new ideas are there?"
- "What would stop this working?"

and if it went well say to yourself...

"I DIDIT!"

and if it could have gone better you can say to yourself...

"I tried a GO FOR IT!"

and if you really believe things are different, having tried the recipes, then let me know.

kevin m thomson

now turn over to... www.thecompanyculturecookbook.com

www.thecompanyculturecookbook.com

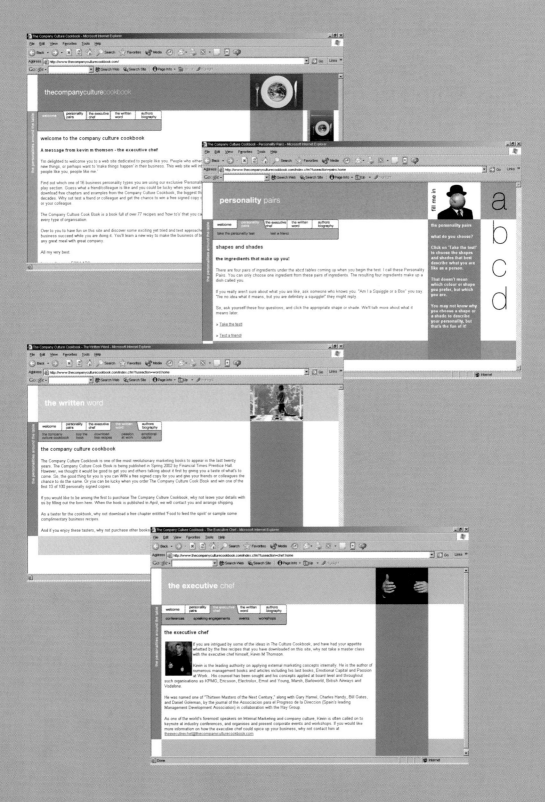

and finally...

Now it's time to visit **www.thecompanyculturecookbook.com** online and begin to make your own recipes for success at work and at home.

Test your personality type, or those of your friends and colleagues. Why not set up a database of all your work partners by personality type and assemble teams using the shape sorter.

Send individualized e-mails, we've called me2u-mails™, to colleagues, friends and family. Talk to me about cooking up a storm in business with your very own company culture cookbook and, who knows, maybe have one of your recipes in *the company culture cookbook part 2*.

Good cooking.

and finally...

More power to your

[business-mind]

Even at the end there's more we can learn. More that *we* can learn from your experience of this book, and more ways to add to *your* learning experience.

For who to read, what to know and where to go in the world of business, visit us at **business-minds.com**.

Here you can find out more about the people and ideas that can make you and your business more innovative and productive. Each month our e-newsletter, *Business-minds Express*, delivers an infusion of thought leadership, guru interviews, new business practice and reviews of key business resources directly to you. Subscribe for free at

▶ **www.business-minds.com/goto/newsletters**

Here you can also connect with ways of putting these ideas to work. Spreading knowledge is a great way to improve performance and enhance business relationships. If you found this book useful, then so might your colleagues or customers. If you would like to explore corporate purchases or custom editions personalised with your brand or message, then just get in touch at

▶ **www.business-minds.com/corporatesales**

We're also keen to learn from your experience of our business books – so tell us what you think of this book and what's on *your* business mind with an online reader report at business-minds.com. Together with our authors, we'd like to hear more from you and explore new ways to help make these ideas work at

▶ **www.business-minds.com/goto/feedback**

[**www.business-minds.com**
www.financialminds.com]